Hope for Change

God's Perfect Plan For Marriage

Suzan Zbell

LifeSource Publishing
Crown Point, Indiana

ISBN: 0-9675987-5-3

Library of Congress Catalog Card Number
00-108960

Scripture quotations marked (AMP) are taken from the Amplified Bible, Old Testament, Copyright 1965, 1987 by the Zondervan Corporation.

The Amplified New Testament, copyright 1954, 1958, 1987 by The Lockman Foundation. Used by permission.

Scripture quotations, marked (NKJ) are taken from the New King James Version. Copyright 1979, 1980, 1982 by Thomas Nelson, Inc. Used by permission. All rights reserved.

Definitions are from Webster's Third New International Unabridged, Seven Language Dictionary, Encyclopedia Britannica, Inc.

Printed in Canada

P.O. Box 471, Crown Point, Indiana, 46307
219-661-0524
www.lifesourcepublishing.com

Acknowledgments

I want to acknowledge and thank the people who have made the principles regarding marriage in the Word of God, life to me. First of all, I thank the Holy Spirit of God for drawing me to Jesus and then bringing revelation of the Word to me. I extend heartfelt thanks to Patti Korzeniewski who first introduced me to God's truth regarding marriage. Then thanks go to our senior pastor, Ronald Johnson Sr., and his wife Carol for teaching, guiding, and overseeing me these many years.

I thank God for my husband, Richard, who has been my strongest supporter over the years. His steadfastness and supernatural faith have continually encouraged me.

Also, I want to extend my heartfelt gratitude to Lesa Woods for editing the manuscript. Her help was vital to the completion of this book. The Preface of this book is a beautiful poem written by Lori Alicea . She has blessed us with her gift of writing many times. Thanks go to Lori Alicea for her contribution to the book.

Thank you God for eternally changing the lives of all who read this book.

Table of Contents

Introduction

To continue to do things the same way over and over with the same results and to expect change is my definition of insanity. This was me for the first 25 years of my marriage. During those years I used to think, "Is this all there is to life and to marriage." In fact there was even a popular song at that time called "Is this all there is?" Then God came into my life and gave me hope. Hope that things could change. Hope for an exciting, fulfilling marriage. A marriage designed in heaven. A definition of hope is a desire accompanied by expectation of, or belief in fulfillment of that expectation. My hopes were more than fulfilled. God is no respecter of persons. What He did for me and what He did for hundreds of other women He will do for you. The only requirement is obedience.

This book is a detailed, comprehensive and instructive look at the glorious plan God has for a woman in marriage. The woman has a distinct, important role to play in marriage. Without the woman fulfilling her role, her husband will never be complete, nor will he be able to fulfill his role.

I have seen these principles change the lives of hundreds of women. This book is based entirely on the Word of God. When something is revealed as truth, it remains truth forever. We can talk around it, dance around it, and do whatever else we want to around it, but it still

remains truth. My prayer is that you will join the hundreds of other women who have embraced this truth, and will allow it to become reality in your life.

There is a thread of three principles found in scripture, running consistently through this book. The first principle is that all truth will be revealed to us by the Spirit of Truth.

> 1 John 2:24-27 NKJ "Therefore let that abide in you which you heard from the beginning. If what you heard from the beginning abides in you, you also will abide in the Son and in the Father. And this is the promise that He has promised us -- eternal life. These things I have written to you concerning those who try to deceive you. But the anointing which you have received from Him abides in you, and you do not need that anyone teach you; but as the same anointing teaches you concerning all things, and is true, and is not a lie, and just as it has taught you, you will abide in Him."

Jesus Christ and His anointing through the Holy Spirit resides within born-again, spirit-filled believers. The Holy Spirit is our teacher and will instruct us in all truth. We have to ask Him for this revelation. An important premise of this book is that in all areas that we lack wisdom, knowledge or understanding, all we have to do is ask our teacher, the Holy Spirit and He will instruct us. Of course we must be obedient to the things He shows us.

The second principle is the principle of sowing and reaping. Your tree may have some really bad fruit on it now, but as you begin to sow good seed in your marriage, good fruit will begin to come forth. The good fruit will actually push the bad fruit off of your tree. If you don't sow seed, you will never have that harvest come forth.

Watch a farmer work in his field. He sows his seed, waters it, fertilizes it and then harvests it. Once in a while he leaves a field unplanted. Nothing comes up in that field but weeds, the same is true in your marriage. So be a wise woman, and begin to sow good seed in your marriage field. My prayer is that you will have a bountiful harvest.

Galatians 6:7-9 NKJ "Do not be deceived, God is not mocked; for whatever a man sows, that he will also reap. For he who sows to his flesh, will of the flesh reap corruption, but he who sows to the Spirit will of the Spirit reap everlasting life. And let us not grow weary while doing good, for in due season we shall reap if we do not lose heart."

The third principle is that you must be a doer of the Word, not just a hearer of the Word. You can read the Word and receive divine inspiration, read wonderful books, hear great sermons, and sit in on revelatory teachings. If you do not put into practice what God shows you, you then will be nothing more than a spiritually stuffed, discouraged woman, wondering, "why is everyone else getting victory and not me"? It could be because they understood they had to be doers and not just hearers of the Word. So my exhortation to you is, be quick to change as God reveals things you need to do to sanctify your marriage.

James 1:21-25 NKJ "Therefore lay aside all filthiness and overflow of wickedness, and receive with meekness the implanted word, which is able to save your souls. But be doers of the Word, and not hearers only, deceiving yourselves. For if anyone is a hearer of the Word and not a doer, he is like a man observing his natural face in a mirror, for he observes himself, goes away, and immediately forgets what

kind of man he was. But he who looks into the
perfect law of liberty and continues in it, and is not a
forgetful hearer but a doer of the Word, this one will
be blessed in what he does."

As you go through the pages of this book, allow the Holy
Spirit to minister life to you. Your obedience to God's
instruction to women, will bring revival into your marriage.
God expects us to make the sacrifice of obedience to the
best of our ability, and He does the rest. God's heart beats
with a passionate desire for sanctified marriages, as our
marriages are a microcosm on earth of the marriage of
Jesus and His Bride. May God bless you abundantly as you
begin your journey of change.

Suzan Zbell

By Lori Alicea

A cup of coffee in my hand,
My cat lays at my side.
A midday moment as I watch,
The quiet life outside.

The squirrels are busy gathering nuts,
And safely tuck away.
The birds have journeyed southern flights,
In search a warmer day.

The flow'rs have given all they have,
'Till spring, no blooms I'll see.
But watching all the leaves that change,
Has so reminded me.

How once the season of my life,
It wasn't spring at all.
The leaves from my own tree turned brown,
And one-by-one they'd fall.

So different from the days gone past,
When fruitful life I found.
Then seasons changed and all my leaves,
They crumbled to the ground.

The nakedness, this tree of mine,
How soon would spring be here?
What hopelessness to be exposed,
When winds of cold are near.

It's sure the winter snow will fall,
As sure as all the leaves.
The promise of the summer sun,
Will shine if you believe.

But while enduring bitter winds,
Create in you a song.
The tree my Father God designed,
Had roots to hold me strong.

Through times it seems my tree will sway,
No hope that I can see.
My faithful Father promised spring,
He so reminded me.

1

The Testimony

I was 21 and Richard was 23 when we got married. He had graduated from college and was on his way to a successful career. I had an excellent position with a major corporation and enjoyed my work, but I lived for the weekends and having fun was my priority. We had lots of friends, did lots of fun things, and we seemed to be very compatible.

I was attracted to Richard because of his stability. He was attracted to me because I was so much fun and had so many friends. He was established in his career at a very young age and I knew he would be a good provider and a stable influence. He was secure and knew where he was going. Me, I just lived life one day at a time, with lots of friends and as much activity as I could squeeze into a day. I thrived in a "Grand Central Station" atmosphere. Richard, on the other hand, thrived in a quiet, sedate atmosphere. The "opposites attract" rule was true for our marriage.

We enjoyed each other; had a good time together, and our families were pleased with our relationship. Did we love each other? Good question. To the degree that we understood love, we did. But love is one of those things that unless you understand the Word of God, you can only love through the clouded position of past relationships and experiences in your family setting. To love each other as the Bible teaches is another matter. We did not have that kind of love at that time. Praise God we do now.

Our wedding was beautiful. My parents were fun people too, with lots of friends, so we had a gala affair with 500 guests. I remember feeling that it was the most perfect day of my life. To say I was ecstatically happy was an understatement. We had a delightful honeymoon in Florida and life seemed almost too perfect. We returned from Florida to a beautifully furnished apartment. It was filled with all the lovely gifts and accessories we had so carefully selected. Most young people, at least not in Ohio where we came from, had their newlywed life as perfectly established as we did. I know now that it was too perfect and we really had too much. We didn't struggle for anything. Struggling together early in your marriage bonds and binds you. In looking back, I can truly say that we never did bond or bind together until much later in our marriage.

Three weeks after the wedding, reality hit and the honeymoon was over. I remember the day. We woke up and felt like we were married to strangers. I wanted the fun and great time to continue and he wanted to settle into the serious business of living. I felt we were supposed to go out and have fun all the time. I wanted to have people over often and relax on weekend mornings. My motto was "work hard, play hard". I believed, "live each day to the fullest as you don't know how many you would have."

Richard held a different opinion of living. He wanted to come home from work, eat dinner and plop down on the couch. Doing this with as little conversation as possible made it that much better. He did not like a lot of excitement or activity in his life. We still were busy on the weekends with lots of plans. After all, what was a weekend without filling it to overflowing with things to do? I found out years later that

Richard hated all that activity and here I thought we were having fun.

One of the biggest reasons for our early marriage problems were our different personalities. Recently, I was watching a television program with Florence Littauer that explained why we had such a difficult time. She was describing the differences between her personality and her husband Fred's. They are direct opposite personality types just as Richard and I. She is an outgoing *Sanguine* personality and her husband is a perfectionist-detailed *Melancholy* personality. After marriage, they found out, just as we did, that they too were married to strangers. They spent years, trying to change one another with no success. You see, our husbands were drawn to fun-loving happy girls, and they couldn't understand why married life wasn't serious enough, perfect enough, or quiet enough. And we on the other hand, having been drawn to quiet, stable, serious men, could not handle the structure and the boredom.

A very interesting study for all of us, especially for married couples is the basic personality types. There are several good books that can be purchased at your Christian Bookstore. I'm recommending *Personality Plus* and other books by Fred and Florence Littauer. Here are some positive and negative traits of the two personalities mentioned in the above paragraph.

Sanguine personalities' positive traits are that they are extroverts, talkers, optimists, and are good on stage. They live in the present and have appealing personalities. They are the life of the party with a good sense of humor. In addition to being enthusiastic and expressive, cheerful and bubbling over, they will physically hold on to their listener. They are childlike, curious, wide-eyed and innocent, sincere at heart with a changeable disposition. That's me. Doesn't sound too bad, does it?

Unfortunately a *Sanguine* personality has some negative traits too, such as brassy, undisciplined, repetitious, forgetful and interruptive. Also, there's a side of this personality that is unpredictable, haphazard, permissive, naïve and gets angry easily. There's also a tendency to be talkative, disorganized, inconsistent, messy, and changeable. Then this personality wants credit, is loud, scatterbrained, restless, and can be a show-off. Doesn't sound too good, does it?

Let's now look at my husband's positive perfect *Melancholy* traits. A person with a strong *Melancholy* personality is deep and thoughtful, (an introvert and a thinker). They are analytical, serious and purposeful and frequently they are genius prone. Some additional attributes are that they are talented and creative, artistic or musical, philosophical and poetic, and appreciative of beauty. They are idealistic, conscientious, self-sacrificing and sensitive to others. Doesn't this sound like a perfect husband?

Some of the negative traits of the *Melancholy* personality are bashful, unforgiving, resentful, fussy, insecure, unpopular, hard-to please and pessimistic. They have negative attitudes, are withdrawn, depressed, introverted, moody and too sensitive. Also, they are alienated, skeptical, a loner, suspicious, revengeful and critical. Does this sound like fun or what?[1]

Because of our different personalities, our husbands felt we really needed a lot of help in order to become "properly adjusted" people. They set out to help us with a steady dose of corrective criticism. In their perfect, orderly way they knew the right way to do everything. Richard is an engineer, so he likes everything to be methodical and exact. It didn't take long until I began to think everything about me was wrong. My joy disappeared, my zest for life disappeared, and I never smiled anymore. I became quite depressed. All I wanted to do was to get away — run away, but I had nowhere to go.

When I got married, my mother said, "You are married for life. There is no divorce; you may never come home to live after you are married, just work it out."

I began to feel I was slipping emotionally. I truly believe that about 1-½ years into my marriage I had an emotional breakdown. There was nowhere I could go nor anyone I could talk to about what I was experiencing. I tried to change to be what Richard expected me to be, but nothing I did was good enough. When watching that TV program, Florence Littauer expressed having the same experience. She said she was forced into developing a "false *Melancholy* personality". She told of her years of misery in not being able to be herself.

I must note here that if you talked to my husband, he would probably have a similar story. I am sure that I was busy trying to change him; criticizing him for not being essentially like me. Amazing, in ignorance, what we do to each other in marriage. In the book of Hosea in the Bible there is a scripture that says, "My people perish for lack of knowledge (or understanding)."

Over the next few years we grew farther apart. We began to get involved in separate activities. Soon Richard was seldom home. He worked long hours and then after work went to a friend's house and built racecars. I had a lot of friends and activities and I was at home as little as possible. We built a large home but spent little time in it. Additional stress was put on our early years with the deaths of close family members. My father died of cancer, his father died of a heart attack/stroke and then my mother died of cancer.

After six years of this estranged marriage, we adopted our first child. I remember the woman at the Social Service Agency saying we were the ideal couple for child placement. She loved us and felt we had everything going for us. She saw us as a young, attractive, educated couple with good jobs,

a beautiful home and excellent reputations in our hometown. I remember feeling like such a phony and thinking, "if she only knew how miserable I am." At that time I felt I could not discuss my problems with anyone. I believed I had to be perfect and could never let anyone know that anything was wrong.

Adopting our son Jim was the most wonderful thing that ever happened to us. For a while it seemed that he was going to make our marriage stronger. But as many people have found out, a child does not solve your marital problems. By now, my husband was home less and less. We had a decent income and although I never abused it, I was able to do whatever I wanted. Richard went to work and earned the money and I did everything else. This system seemed to work for us.

Without our even having applied for another child the Adoption Agency, still feeling that we were their "ideal" adoptive parents, called us one day. They said they had a child they felt would be the "perfect brother" for our baby Jimmy. We were blessed with our second child, John. Shortly before the adoption my youngest sister moved in with us and we really had a "Grand Central Station" existence. It was even too Grand Central for me. When I think of all these things happening and my husband's dislike for commotion, I cannot even imagine how miserable he must have been.

For a while things seemed more tolerable, but we were still growing apart. He lost himself in his work and often stopped at a watering hole afterwards. I devoted myself to raising my children. He wasn't happy at work, so he sought other employment and we moved to the Detroit, Michigan area. We lived there for seven years. I loved those years. We made wonderful friends and were constantly busy, going on small recreational trips and doing very healthy things. That area is very much geared to outdoor activities and it had a great family atmosphere.

We were blessed with finally being able to conceive a child and had twin boys, Jeff and Joe. It was hard. Richard still worked and I did everything else. There was no family to help me, but I loved my children and enjoyed my life of taking care of them. However, I did have many other young mothers with children the same ages as ours for friends. We did things with our children every day. When our children started playing hockey we had a family activity that we all shared equally. It seemed like things were finally getting better.

We moved into a larger home in the same area in Michigan. We overextended ourselves financially. This was my fault, because I really wanted this home. Eventually, we were not making it financially and my husband looked for a new job. This one was in Pittsburgh, Pennsylvania. We had a home built there and moved. The move to Pittsburgh was very hard on our oldest son, Jim, because his little life was really getting established in Michigan. For me, it was one of the hardest things I had to do. In Michigan, for the first time in my life, I had been happy. Richard and I had to drive separate cars to Pittsburgh and I remember driving down our street for the last time. I experienced a devastating sadness and a desperation of loss of family. We had all truly become each other's family. There was nothing we wouldn't do for one another. We had been similar people with similar needs and we just fit together. There were a lot of us and we weren't just friends, we were one big, happy family. As I write this I still feel sad, and I still feel the loss.

After we got established in Pittsburgh, Richard told me that he never wanted to get involved with people like that again. I thought he had loved Michigan as I had. But he was miserable for those seven years. He did not want the social activities, friendships, and commitments, like we had there ever again. What I thought had been okay I found out was not, and to this day I've not gotten involved with people in that manner. As I'm writing this, my eyes fill with tears, as I sense the loss of close relationships. But now, my relationship with the Lord fills all the voids in my life.

We were in Pittsburgh for one year, and then Richard was offered his job back with his original company in Youngstown, Ohio, our hometown. They made him an offer he couldn't refuse and we moved to a lovely home in Poland, Ohio. Ohio was nice as we were near family. Our marriage was status quo — he worked, I did everything else — minimal communication — involved with kids' sports etc. By now though, the older boys were getting a little harder to handle. I had always disciplined the kids and didn't even know how to include Richard. When He did get involved, he felt my resistance to him and overreacted, so we had a no win situation. I needed his help, but didn't know how to get it. He wanted to get involved, but didn't know how. We really were a mess. But if you looked at us from the outside, we still looked good.

After two years in Ohio we were transferred to Indiana. Ironically, each time we moved, we felt it was the answer for our lives. This change would be good for us and would make everything right. Wrong! Years ago I heard a saying "there is no geographical cure for your problems" and I can truly, through experience, confirm that statement.

Shortly after the move to Indiana, I was in a state of depression. My husband moved there for a particular job. Soon after we arrived that job was taken from him and he was given a different job. Three years later I found out that had been the root cause of my depression. All these moves and nothing was ever what it seemed it was going to be.

Two schools in Michigan, one in Pennsylvania, one in Ohio and now a new school in Indiana was just one too many for our older boys. They had no stability in their lives. Since they changed schools so many times in the early elementary years, they had missed some of the basics. School became progressively more difficult for them.

Their lives were filled with insecurity. The circumstances surrounding their births and subsequent adoptions, the moves and school changes, Richard's absence, and my depression all led to this insecurity. They saw their parents living separate lives and not displaying open love and affection, and this made matters even worse.

As the boys grew older they became more and more rebellious — I became more and more desperate. Throughout most of my marriage I suffered from severe anxiety attacks. During this time they became worse and fear began to rule my life. Out of necessity Richard would try to discipline the boys. He had not been involved in disciplining them before, and when he did, it seemed extreme. I would get involved and counter what he did. This, of course, was the worst thing I could have done. It allowed them to be more rebellious. Then through my fear, I began to control everything so that all my ships would stay afloat. The only problem was that they were not staying afloat — they were sinking. The most amazing thing was that if you looked at us you would think that we were the perfect family.

Things escalated with the boys, our marriage grew more distant, and I became more bitter, angry and fearful. I began to really hate my husband, but felt I was stuck in this marriage forever. I believed if I took my kids and got out everything would be fine. My husband and I did not communicate, except for essentials. He never came home until late at night. This was a combination of work and watering holes. Richard was very successful at work and that's where he liked to spend his time. That's where he got his strokes. I remember thinking one day, how awful it was that our only need of him was a paycheck. It was a barren life.

It wasn't long after this that I went to the doctor for a check up and he told me I had cancer. I had surgery and was told I would need two years of chemotherapy. In the hospital, before surgery, an IV Therapist witnessed to me in a way that touched my heart and I understood. I received the Lord. I had been seeking out the reality of God for two years. (God was in charge of this though, for that morning on the way to work, the Lord spoke to her and told her to witness to the first patient she went to that day.) I had a visitation of the Holy Spirit that night. I knew that the surgery would reveal cancer and I would have to undergo chemotherapy. I also knew that I would be completely healed. I felt that this was pretty good for only being saved one day.

All of the above happened, including the healing. All praise to God!

I thought my life had been barren before, but those two years of chemotherapy were the most barren, lonely years of my life. Back then cancer was something no one wanted to talk about. I would try to talk about it, but no one would listen. So I stuffed my feelings. All my life I stuffed my feelings deep down inside.

Those years found the older boys acting out, the younger boys watching and our lives disintegrating even faster. I remember daily telling myself, that I could not continue like this. When the two years of chemo were up, I was taking the boys and getting an apartment. By then I had a part time job. I knew that I could turn it into a full time job.

I'm not going to go into additional details other than to say that during this two-year period my younger sister who lived in Washington, D. C. was brutally murdered. She had been the only link of support I had after my surgery. After my chemo ended I went on a 40-day journey with God. I decided to do this prior to leaving and getting an apartment for the boys and myself. I went to church and asked God everyday to reveal Himself to me. At the end of this time, I received the Baptism of the Holy Spirit and I was introduced to teaching on how to be a "Godly Wife" according to scripture. God really tricked me. I asked Him to reveal Himself to me and He did!

The cure for my problems began with receiving Jesus Christ into my life and then allowing Him to begin the process of change in me. It's amazing how people deceive themselves into believing that things, places, and even other people can change the disturbed areas in their lives. I praise God that He found me and showed me that He is the only way, the only truth and the only life.

I began a daily journey of revelation and change that is still going on. I minister to women by teaching all that God did, and all the things He still does to me, for me and through me. I've seen hundreds and hundreds of women released from their prisons into glorious Christ-centered lives, overcoming the obstacles before them, and then reaching out and touching others. That's what it's all about; being touched and then reaching out and touching others.

This is a thumb-nail-sketch of my 25-year prison experience. I was in a prison of my own making. But today I dwell in the Palace with the King of Kings and the Lord of Lords. Won't you trust God to release you from the prison and then trust Him to take you to the Palace?

As a little P.S. to this testimony, as God healed me and turned me from the false *Melancholy* to the true *Sanguine* I began to flourish. He took away all the negative traits of the personality and restored the positive ones. Also, God transformed my precious husband Richard into a wonderfully balanced *Melancholy*. Of course we are more than just one personality trait. I used to not like these labels, but when I realized it was God's plan for us and He had no trouble with them, I began to enjoy and appreciate them. God is so good to us. He works so hard to chip off those rough edges. He is patient. To Him I give all the glory and praise for our changed lives.

I never knew that God had a perfect plan for marriage until I was married for 25 years and was the "ripe young" age of 46. At that time our boys were 19, 18 and our twins were 14 years old. We were in the throes of experiencing four teenage boys. It was quite a challenge. We survived and are now the parents of four extraordinary men. The two oldest are married to beautiful young women and each has a son and a daughter. Our twins are not yet married, so we have the joy of more daughters-in-law and, of course, of more grandchildren to come. At this stage of our lives, we enjoy a close adult friendship with our sons and their wives and are delighting in our grandchildren.

Everyone has a testimony. Yours may not be the same as mine, but nonetheless you may be like me, in a place that you know is not "heaven on earth". God intends for our marriages to be a representation of "heaven on earth". A husband and wife relationship is the earthly representation of Jesus and the Church. In the book of Revelation the sanctified church is called the "Bride of Christ". When Jesus comes to earth for the second time, He is coming for His Bride, the sanctified, Body of Christ. He will take His Bride and put her into His side, right where He was pierced for her the first time and where the blood flowed, and He will join her with Him and they shall become one for all eternity.

God wants to sanctify (cleanse and purify) your marriage, and take you and place you into the side of your husband and make you one for all eternity. When the Word of God says, "they shall be joined together and become one", it means just that.

Are you willing to begin on this exciting journey that will radically change your life, change your marriage and bring you into a place of peace and contentment?

If you are, then pray the following prayer:

P   *Dear Lord, I'm ready for change. Forgive me that through ignorance, (or false information), or even through rebellion I have not been the*
R   *wife I should have been to my husband. I take the precious blood of Jesus and I cover my sin.*
A   *Repent means to turn away from and change. This day I commit to turn away from my incor-*
Y   *rect behavior, actions and attitudes. Right now I'm not sure of what's going to take place, but I*
E   *choose to trust you. Today I make a quality decision, a decision that I'm not going to turn back*
R   *from, but I am going to be obedient to the things you show me that I need to do to change. Please only give me what I can manage day-by-day. I will trust you each day. I will not put expectations on my husband, but I will trust you to change me. How you deal with my husband is your business, not mine.*

Lord, I thank you and praise you in advance for a sanctified marriage. I Thank you and praise you that we will become one and that I will fit into that place in his side that is prepared for me. Also, thank you that no one but me can fit into that place, a place of completion set aside just for me. Amen.

1. Personality Plus, Florence Littauer, Baker Publishing

2

God's Perfect Plan

Genesis 1:27 - AMP "So God created man in His own image, in the image and likeness of God He created him; male and female He created them."

Genesis 2:21-24 - AMP "And the Lord God caused a deep sleep to fall upon Adam; and while he slept, He took one of his ribs or a part of his side and closed up the (place with) flesh. And the rib or part of his side, which the Lord had taken from the man, He built up and made into a woman and He brought her to the man. Then Adam said, this (creature) is now bone of my bones and flesh of my flesh; she shall be called Woman, because she was taken out of man. Therefore a man shall leave his father and his mother and shall become united and cleave to his wife, and they shall become one flesh."

Matthew 19:5 - AMP "And He (Jesus) said, for this reason a man shall leave his father and mother and shall be united firmly (joined inseparably) to his wife, and the two shall become one flesh."

Ephesians 5:31-33 - AMP "For this reason a man shall leave his father and his mother and shall be joined to his wife, and the two shall become one flesh. This mystery is very great, but I speak concerning (the relation of) Christ and the church. However, let each man of you (without exception) love his wife as (being in a sense) his very own self; and let the wife see that she respects and reverences her husband (that she notices him, regards him honors, him, prefers him, venerates and esteems him); and that she defers to him, praises him and loves and admires him exceedingly."

If you are just beginning your journey of change, and you see how far away you and your mate are from the reality of the above scriptures, you may be thinking, "this sounds great, but my circumstances are so extreme this could never be so for me". If you are thinking this, you are partially right. This could never be so, without God. I can honestly say that I know God works miracles in my life, and in the women into whose lives I've had the privilege of imparting God's plan for marriage. I too felt that it would be impossible for my husband and me to have this kind of marriage. My marriage was bankrupt, physically, spiritually and emotionally.

But God showed up and began a work in my life. Before I begin to share the process of change that took place in me, through the work of the Holy Spirit in my life, I want to give you a sneak preview into the future — your future.

You may look at your husband now and say "man may be created in God's image, but I can't see anything in my husband that is godlike". This may be true, but God sees it differently, for God knows the beginning and the end. God knows what he's like now, but God also knows what He's going to do to and for and with your husband.

When I began to understand God's plan for marriage and began to allow Him to change me, I did not see anything godlike in my husband. Now, and for many years, my husband is known everywhere he goes for his godlike character. He is the spiritual head of our home, he is an elder in our church, a man who is impeccably obedient to the Word of God and who loves and follows Jesus with all his heart. This is certainly a wonderful gift that God has given to me and to our family and to the Body of Christ. There is no denying that he was created in the image and likeness of God. Even though I couldn't see it, God knew all the time that it was there, and God knew just what to do to bring it all into evident existence.

When we look at Genesis 2:21-24 we see that woman came into existence through God causing Adam to rest and then taking a rib from his side. God closed up that place in Adam with flesh, but the rib was still missing. It never says in Genesis that God replaced the rib taken from man with a new one. Adam had a void or a part missing until God completed Eve. Adam had an incomplete spot in his side, a spot that was arched out and curved. How strange it would feel knowing that suddenly you are incomplete. When you got married, your husband was made complete by you. The incomplete, arched out and curved spot in his side was made whole when he married you. No other woman will ever fit into that spot. That is your place and your place alone. That's why it is so important for marriages to become healthy.

"Then God took the rib or part of Adam's side and he built it up and made it into a woman and then brought her to the man." To build up means to develop gradually by increments, to promote the health, strength, esteem or reputation of, to accumulate or develop appreciably.

Perhaps like me, in order for you to become that woman

God wants to take and place back into the correct position in your husband, you might need some building up. God really astounded me when he began to show me that I was the one who was going to have to change. It wasn't that my husband didn't need to change, but God had my full attention so he started with me. It only takes one to change a whole family.

For two years I stopped looking at the faults in my husband, and focused on God and me. At the same time I was fully persuaded that God could take care of my husband. By the end of two years, a transformation had taken place in my husband. He became a "Man of God".

The Word of God became flesh in my life. What I mean is it became reality for me. I understood it and was living it. It was this obedience to the Word and my willingness to die to my own desire that produced this change. All this occurred because of the grace of God. It was not something I could have worked up on my own or achieved by an act of my will. Apart from the Holy Spirit I had no chance. The following scripture is the one that God showed me had become life and the reality of the Word becoming flesh in our lives. The scripture verse was 1 Corinthians 7:14.

> "For the unbelieving husband is sanctified by the wife, and the unbelieving wife is sanctified by the husband; otherwise your children would be unclean, but now they are holy."

- ◆ Sanctify - to set apart to a sacred purpose or religious use (consecrate); to free from sin (purity); to make productive of holiness or piety

God revealed to me that He was doing the same thing in both of us, but He was not doing it the exact same way. God

is going to work in your life the way He knows is the very best for you. All you have to do is be obedient to the things that He shows you. It may be the same way it worked for us, but it probably won't be. You're unique and God wants to work His perfect work through your uniqueness.

God brought me to my husband and I fit perfectly into that spot in his side that was mine alone. We were so different. I could not have imagined it could ever have been so. But with God all things are possible. God brought a miracle into our lives. At the end of two years we were not perfect, but we were so much better and getting better by leaps and bounds. The glorious reality with God is that He's never done changing us. It is a continual process. In reality, the change that took place during those two years was only the beginning. The staring place is the point of realization that it's God's perfect plan for a man and a woman to be married. He changes us so that we can come together correctly. God can display His glory, for His Name's sake through the changed marriage. The most exciting news is that He never leaves things in a stagnant stage, but is always desiring that more and more of His glory be displayed. As the scripture tells us:

> 2 Corinthians 3:17-18 - AMP "Now the Lord is the Spirit, and where the Spirit of the Lord is, there is liberty (emancipation from bondage, freedom). And all of us, as with unveiled face, (because we) continued to behold (in the Word of God) as in a mirror the glory of the Lord, are constantly being transfigured into His very own image in ever increasing splendor and from one degree of glory to another; (for this comes) from the Lord (Who is) the Spirit."

In being transfigured into His very own image and in

being placed in proper position into and with our husbands, we are getting back to the oneness that God planned from the beginning, at creation.

> Genesis 1:27 - AMP "So God created man in His own image, in the image and likeness of God He created him: MALE AND FEMALE He created them."

Are you ready? God wants to begin a process of setting you free to be who He says you are, not whom someone else or the world says you are.

> Isaiah 61:1 - AMP "The Spirit of the Lord God is upon me, because the Lord has anointed and qualified me to preach the Gospel of good tidings to the meek, the poor, and afflicted; He has sent me to bind up and heal the brokenhearted, to proclaim liberty to the (physical and spiritual) captives and the opening of the prison and of the eyes to those who are bound."

P
R
A
Y
E
R

Dear Lord, I thank you that you care so much about each one of us. Teach us how to love You more and more. Teach me how to read and study Your Word. Please let me see myself, and not my husband, not others, as You begin to show me areas through Your Word, Your teachers, Your preachers and my Pastor, that need changed in me. I proclaim physical and spiritual liberty in my life and my family's life. Order my steps oh Lord, so that I'm where you want me to be, and that I hear what you want me to hear, see what you want me to see. I trust You to set up circumstances for me to be released from my prison or prisons.

Lord, I desire to bring glory to Your name through my marriage. May people be drawn to You and give You all praise as they see the changes in our lives. I thank you and praise you for this in the Name of Jesus. Amen.

3

Divorce - Breaking Asunder

M en and women hurt and sometimes even destroy each other in marriage. It is amazing to think that God wants marriage to be a blessing, yet many couples feel that their marriage is a curse. Since marriage is a picture of the relationship between Jesus and His Bride, (the Church), can you just imagine how this must break His heart.

You may be married, but in your heart you have divorced your husband. If you are not connecting and simply co-exist in the same house, but in all reality living separate lives, you have entered into a spiritual divorce. If you spend a great deal of your time giving each other the silent treatment, ignoring each other and wishing you could get out of your mess, you have entered into a silent divorce.

Take time before the Lord and examine your heart. Is there a part in you that wants to run? Do you really feel you want out of your marriage? Does it seem like it is going to be too much of an effort to work on your marriage? If you answered yes to any or all of these questions or could answer yes to any similar questions, you are harboring divorce in your heart. Today, when there is difficulty in a marriage, immediately thoughts and words go to divorce. It is essential that the "D" word be removed from your vocabulary and from your heart. (Your mouth speaks forth the issues of your heart.)

When a man and woman enter into marriage, they enter into a covenant with each other and God. God keeps His covenant with us in all areas and He expects us to keep covenant with Him.

The word covenant is defined as an agreement that is usually formal, solemn, and intended as binding.

Today people do not have "fear of the Lord". When one wants out of a marriage, in effect they are rebelling against the covenant they made with God. If a mate takes circumstances into his hands and leaves his wife, there still needs to be total reliance upon God for restoration. Even in that extreme scenario, God is able to perform a miracle. He can do all things. He knows He can do all things. Our problem is we don't believe He can.

God hates divorce. It's a tearing and ripping of "one flesh". The binding commitment of marriage is not dependant upon what man wills or what either individual does or doesn't do, but it depends upon the design that God originally intended for marriage. Let's take a look at Gomer and Hosea.

Hosea 3:1-3 - AMP "Then the Lord said to me, go again, love (the same) woman (Gomer) who is beloved of a paramour and is an adulteress, even as the Lord loves the children of Israel, though they turn to other gods and love cakes of raisons (used in the sacrificial feasts in idol worship). So I bought her for fifteen pieces of silver and a homer and a half of barley, (the price of a slave). And I said to her, you shall be betrothed to me for many days; you shall not play the harlot and you shall not belong to another man. So will I also be to you (until you have proved your loyalty to me and our marital relations may be resumed)."

This was to be a time of rebuilding trust.

Following is an article from the Women's study Bible, N. J. Nelson Publishers: 2.

God rejects Divorce
for the following reasons:

1. Marriage is a divine institution (covenant) that the Lord used to teach His children about their relationship to Him. (Genesis 1:27 - NKJ "So God created man in His own image, in the image of God He created Him, male and female He created them.")

No other human relationship, not with parent or with child, is to supersede the bond between husband and wife. Marriage is a covenant commitment, -a vow made to God and the partner, not only to love but also to be faithful and to endure in this lifelong exclusive relationship.

Marriage is a threefold miracle.

a) A biological miracle by which two people actually become one flesh.

b) A social miracle through which two families are grafted together.

c) A spiritual miracle in that the marriage relationship pictures the union of Christ and His Bride.

2. Marriage is by express command of the Creator and carries His signature.

3. Marriage brings two people together as one flesh, testifying to the permanence God planned for this most intimate union.

4. Jesus points to the example of the first couple.

5. Evil consequences are inevitable when separation comes.

Divorce is never God's choice.
Indeed, God hates divorce.

Malachi 2:16 NKJ "For the Lord God of Israel says, that He hates divorce, for it covers one's garment with violence, says the Lord of Hosts. Therefore take heed to your spirit that you do not deal treacherously."

However, whenever divorce occurs, for whatever reason, God desires to work redemptively when the person who has experienced this tragedy is repentant and desires reconciliation to God.

Today approximately half of all Christian marriages end in divorce. If you have been divorced and are remarried, know that God is forgiving and redeeming. He desires you to start right now, at the place you are at this moment, to begin to believe for a brand new relationship with your mate. Cry out for God to circumcise your marriage; for Him to cut off the old dead areas of your marriage. Ask Him to give you a new marriage, one that will actually be made in Heaven, by Him. He did this for me and for countless others we have worked with. He did this also for those all over the world who were willing to trust Him with their marriages. I'm sure you've tried a lot of things, and the results have not been lasting.

Our God is in the marriage counseling business, let Him be your teacher, let Him show you the way. He is able to give you above and beyond anything you could ever imagine.

Following is a prayer of affirmation that you need to make regarding your marriage. This is a prayer that needs to be prayed more than once. It would be good to pray this daily until you get a release from the Holy Spirit that the battle has been won in the heavenlies. Then stand, and above all else stand, until you see the reality in the natural. This prayer was given to me a few years ago. I don't know who originated it, but it says it all.

Dear Lord, I speak forth the following proclamation. I am standing for the healing of my marriage. I will not give up, give in, give out, or give over until healing takes place. I made a vow, I gave the pledge, I gave a ring, I took a ring, I gave myself, and I trusted God and said the words. I meant the words "in sickness and in health, in sorrow and in joy, for better or for worse, for richer or for poorer, in good times and in bad until death do us part", so I am standing now and will not sit down, fall down, back down, or be down until the breakdown is torn down. I refuse to put my eyes on outward circumstances, or listen to prophets of doom, or buy into what is trendy, worldly, popular, convenient or easy, quick, thrifty or advantageous. Nor will I settle for a cheap imitation of God's real thing. Nor will I seek to lower God's standard, twist God's will, re-write God's Word, violate God's covenant, or accept what God hates ... namely divorce.

In a world of sin, I will stay pure. Surrounded by lies, I will speak the truth. Where hopelessness abounds, I will hope in God; where revenge is easier, I will bless instead of curse and where the odds are stacked against me, I will trust in God's faithfulness.

I am a stander and I will not acquiesce, compromise, quarrel or quit. I have made the choice, set my face, entered the race, believed the Word and trusted God for the outcome.

I will allow neither the reaction of my spouse, or the urging of my friends, nor the advice of my loved ones, nor economic hardship, nor the prompting of the devil, to make me let up, slow up, blow up, or give up until my marriage is healed. I proclaim this in Jesus' name. Amen.

2. Women's Study Bible, N. J. Nelson Publishers, page 1615.

4

Healing the Wounded Spirit

Marriage is two becoming one flesh. In the most ideal state it's being connected at every level. If you are struggling in your marriage, and feel that there is a wall between you and your husband that you just can't break through, it is quite possible that he has wounded your spirit. The same is possibly true for him. His spirit could be wounded too. You need to trust God to take care of the wounded spirit in him and be concerned with getting free yourself so that you can minister correctly to your husband.

Jeremiah 30:17 - NKJ "For I will restore health to you and heal you of your wounds, says the Lord, because they called you an outcast saying this is Zion; no one seeks her."

Proverbs 18:14 - NKJ "The spirit of a man will sustain him in sickness, but who can bear a broken spirit."

Look at the following definitions of key words and see if any of them apply to you and your situation:

- Bruise means to inflict, bruise or hurt; to injure; to wound; to damage; A surface injury to flesh or soul

- Wound means an injury or hurt to a person or their feelings or reputation; to mar; to damage; to hurt; to dishonor; to injure; to harm; to spoil

- Broken is defined as flattened; shattered; rent; wrecked; destroyed; reduced; smashed; crushed; ruptured; interrupted; separated

God sees where you are, He knows where you've been and what you've been through, and wants to make a great exchange with you. He wants you to give Him the pain, shame and wounds of your past, and He wants to give you beauty for ashes, the oil of joy for mourning, and the garment of praise for the spirit of heaviness.

Isaiah 61:1-5 NKJ "The Spirit of the Lord God is upon Me, because the Lord has anointed Me to preach good tidings to the poor; He has sent Me to heal the bro-kenhearted, to proclaim liberty to the captives, and opening of the prison to those who are bound; to pro-claim the acceptable year of the Lord, and the day of vengeance of our God; to comfort all who mourn, to console those who mourn in Zion, to give the beauty for ashes, the oil of joy for mourning, the garment of praise for a spirit of heaviness; that they may be called trees of righteousness, the planting of the Lord, that He may be glorified.

And they shall rebuild the old ruins, they shall raise up the former desolations, and they shall repair the ru-ined cities, the desolations of many generations. Strangers shall stand and feed your flocks, and the sons of the foreigner shall be your plowmen and your

vinedressers. But you shall be named the priests of the Lord, they shall call you the servants of our God. You shall eat the riches of the Gentiles, and in their glory you shall boast. Instead of your shame you shall have double honor, and instead of confusion they shall rejoice in their portion. Therefore my own arm brought salvation for Me; and My own fury, it sustained Me.

What a wonderful exchange. God is so wonderful, He takes our messes, heals us and then gives us double honor, and a double portion, all because He loves us, but most of all because He is God and desires all to see His glory displayed in our lives.

If a person has a wounded or bruised spirit, it is because there was a wrong done to them or somehow they were injured. A broken spirit is one's personhood being crushed by life's difficulties. It is frequently accompanied by depression. A wounded spirit is a telltale sign of a "root of bitterness".

Hebrews 12:14-15 - NKJ "Pursue peace with all people and holiness, without which no one will see the Lord, looking carefully lest anyone fall short of the grace of God, lest any root of bitterness springing up cause trouble, and by this many become defiled."

When we are hurt or bruised, something takes place deep on the inside of us; down deep in our soul and spirit, and if the bruising was physical, our bodies. Then, through attempts to get over whatever caused the wounding, we tell ourselves that we're okay, we can handle this; it's over; I'm not upset, etc. But deep down inside there's an open wound. And whenever the enemy of our soul, the devil, desires, he can come and access that wound. The result may be depression, anger, fear, insecurity, rejection and on and on.

If we think the emotional areas mentioned above do not bother our families and those close to us, we are only fooling ourselves. We must come to the realization that a "root" is deep within us and we have to allow the Holy Spirit to expose this root, so that we can be free. Also, we must realize that through these negative emotions there is a spillover of depression, anger, fear, insecurity, and rejection, onto everyone around us. Spouses and children pick up on these things very quickly. Many times women can fool themselves, thinking that all of their emotions are deep within themselves, and not hurting anyone. Precious woman, you are hurting everyone, especially yourself.

If in the past, your husband has hurt you, you must be willing to look at what has taken place so you can give it to God. You must repent for your root of bitterness or "hidden" unforgiveness, saturate the wounded area with the blood of Jesus, and ask God to completely heal you and your wound. Then you need to ask God to heal and restore you and your husband.

God is willing to be gracious to you and forgive you of all your sins, and you need to let go of these wounds and forgive your husband. Walk today in unconditional forgiveness like Jesus did and does.

- Unconditional forgiveness is an act of submitting our will to the will of the Father.

- We know that it is God's will for us to forgive.

- Reflect on the times that God has forgiven you.

Matthew 6:12-15 - NKJ "And forgive us our debts, as we forgive our debtors, and do not lead us into temptation, but deliver us from evil. For yours is the kingdom and the power and the glory forever. Amen. For if you forgive men their trespasses, your heavenly Father will also forgive you. But if you do not forgive men their trespasses, neither will your Father forgive your trespasses."

◆ We've all sinned much and been forgiven much.

◆ Therefore we are to love much.

Luke 7:47 - AMP "Therefore I tell you her sins, many as they are, are forgiven her, because she has loved much. But he who is forgiven little, loves little."

As you look at how you were mistreated you may say, "I can't let go of this. You don't understand and you don't know how badly it hurts." My answer would be, "I don't, but Jesus does." Remember it hurt Him when they whipped and beat Him and then put Him on a cross to die. You probably did not deserve what happened to you, and neither did Jesus deserve what happened to Him. Our response when wronged needs to be the same response that Jesus had.

Luke 23:34 - NKJ "Then Jesus said, Father, forgive them, for they do not know what they do."

P   *Father I come before you today and I ask for your
    forgiveness. Forgive me for the times that I have*
R   *offended and wronged my husband. Lord today I
    choose to forgive my husband for all the times he
    has hurt and wounded me, and abused me ver-*
A   *bally, mentally, or even physically (if necessary).
    I open up the cage I've held him in and I let him*
Y   *out. Father please remove from me the roots of
    bitterness that are growing from my bruised*
E   *areas. Father pour the precious blood of Jesus
    into these areas and allow the healing blood to*
R   *do a complete work. Today, I believe, my wounds
    are healed. Then fill me up with unconditional
    forgiveness, which is your agape love. Let your
    love overflow out of me onto my husband. Al-
    low him to be changed by the power of your
    love. I pray and believe that this will be so, by
    the precious name of Jesus. AMEN.*

Go to your husband and ask him to forgive you for not letting go of your woundedness and allowing a root of bitterness to form. This may seem difficult for some of you to do, and it my even be hard for him to receive, but the truth is He needs to be set free too. He probably knows that something is not quite right, but is not able to identify what it is. Over and over, I have seen this humbling act produce beautiful results.

If you want to give yourself a beautiful gift, go before the Lord and ask Him to show you if you are harboring any unforgiveness towards anyone else. Repent, release them, give them the same gift of forgiveness that Jesus so freely gave you, send them a card and ask them to forgive you if you have ever hurt, wounded or disappointed them in anyway.

(Remember, there was sin in your heart, because you harbored bitterness or woundedness.) Try this; you'll love it, there is great joy in freedom.

The truth of the matter is, as you release people from the cages you've kept them in, you're the one who is set free. They've been happily living their lives and you've been doing all the suffering. Look at it this way, when we allow a root of bitterness to remain, we in effect are allowing the offense to happen to us over and over again. Now that does not make sense. So let's do it God's way. Let it go. Let them go. And set yourself free!!

5

Leave and Cleave

Genesis 2:24 - KJV "Therefore a man shall leave his father and his mother and shall become united and cleave to his wife, and they shall become one flesh."

God's great design for marriage is permanence. Even though there were no parents present, when God spoke the words "a man shall leave his father and his mother and shall become united and cleave to his wife", He was making provision for the future. God made woman from man. In creating woman, God took a rib from man and left him incomplete. A man is made complete when he marries and brings his wife unto himself. Leaving and cleaving is possible only through marriage.

Great damage is done to both men and women that live together before marriage. First of all it's sin. Secondly, there is no commitment nor is there leaving and cleaving. Cohabitation without marriage leaves both man and woman with an easy way out and an attitude of "I'll leave if _____, you fill in the blank. Today 50% of marriages end in divorce and 25% of children are born out of wedlock.

We know that today, the morals are such that men and women, even girls and boys, become sexually involved outside of marriage; some living together without the bond of marriage. Couples can never be satisfied or fulfilled in arrangements like these.

When you marry, you must be willing to lay aside all that pertains to your old lifestyle, old loyalties, old activities, and separate plans and goals. It is important to develop a new lifestyle based on decisions you make together. Your loyalties must be to your spouse; nothing should be allowed to come in and bring division. Guard your marriage and let no one separate you from your husband. Parents are never, never to bring division into the lives of their married children. God is serious about this. (He does not like it.) Plan activities that you can do together. Separate activities should only take place through mutual consent.

Set goals and make decisions together rather than be moved compulsively. When you have agreement in plans and activities you will have a fulfilling marriage. Decisions on where to go to church, tithing, child raising, and finances must be discussed in detail before you are married. Realistically discuss income potential based on his earning capabilities. (I will have a chapter on the tragedy of a woman being forced to work because their lifestyle requires her income after she has a child.) Because God has put a natural maternal instinct into a woman, many times she desperately wants to stay home and nurture and raise her child.

Many couples marry and all they've thought about ahead of time are the plans for the wedding. If you remember from my testimony in Chapter One this is what I did. You wake up a couple of weeks after the wedding and wonder, "who is this person I've married." At that point, you want out and have trouble remembering your wedding vows let alone the principle of "leaving and cleaving". (This is probably how the phrase "the honeymoon is over" originated.)

- Cleave means abide, cling fast together, follow
  close after, be joined together, to stick.

Once you marry, in God's eyes you are inseparable. Two good word pictures of how God sees a married couple is they're bonded together with superglue, or they are laminated together by the laminating machine. I took a picture of my husband and myself and put us back-to-back and laminated the pictures together. If I were to try to separate the two pictures, I would tear apart one or probably both pictures. That's how permanent laminating is. In the eyes of God marriage is much more permanent than laminating.

We have all seen the destruction that accompanies divorce. In a divorce everyone is wounded emotionally. The innocent victims of divorce are children. God's command that we are to "leave and cleave" protects children and builds strong families. Today's children are so confused. Many have no sense of security, permanence, loyalty, or a sense of belonging. These of course are just a few areas of fallout from not following Gods perfect plan. Teachers today have to spend a lot their time parenting, instead of educating, because children are not getting what they need at home.

This is horrendous. God has given the responsibility of instilling values in children to their parents. It is very difficult for a single mom or dad to be both parents. In fact, it is impossible. A lot of the problems in education today are a result of the effects of both parents working, divorce, and parental preoccupation. (This is another area, I'll address later. You can be an absentee parent, even when you're home with your children.)

Understand that everything you do affects your husband and your children. The Word says that through marriage a man and woman are joined together and become one flesh.

If one sins, the other senses that something is wrong. They might not be able to exactly put their finger on what's wrong, but they know something's wrong. God joins man and woman together, not only so that they become one flesh, but He also joins them together spirit-to-spirit. Some people are so pre-occupied that they don't even recognize what's going on. Ask God to make you aware and alert so that if and when your husband's heading for trouble, you can pray.

You might be thinking, "I know that my husband is in trouble.. What can I do?" There is an "umbrella of protection" that God has for women and children who are correctly lined up under their husband's authority. I am not saying that you have to agree with the incorrect thing your husband may be doing. With God's grace, submit yourself to God and ask Him to teach you how to love your husband, how to be obedient to the Word and how to submit to your husband's headship in the home and marriage. God's Word is true, it will not return void and it will never fail. Following the principles in this book will affect change in your marriage.

- ◆ Umbrella - Something which provides protection, as a defensive air cover, as over a battlefront— of protection—an act of covering or shielding from exposure, injury or destruction: to guard: to defend

If your husband is not lined up correctly with God, but you are, even though there is in effect a hole in your umbrella, you and your children will be protected by God, through your act of submission to God and His Word. Following are two portions of scripture for you to hide in your heart.

Ephesians - NKJV 5:21-33 "Submitting to one another in the fear of God. Wives submit to your own husbands, as to the Lord. For the husband is the head of the wife, as also Christ is head of the church and He is the Savior of the body. Therefore, just as the church is subject to Christ, so let the wives be to their own husbands in everything. Husbands, love your wives, just as Christ also loved the church and gave Himself for her, that He might sanctify and cleanse her with the washing of water by the Word, that He might present her to Himself a glorious church, not having spot or wrinkle or any such thing, but that she should be holy and without blemish. So husbands ought to love their own wives as their own bodies. He who loves his wife loves himself. For no one ever hated his own flesh, but nourishes and cherishes it, just as the Lord does the church. For we are members of His body, of His flesh and of His bones. For this reason a man shall leave his father and mother and be joined to his wife, and the two shall become one flesh. This is a great mystery, but I speak concerning Christ and the church. Nevertheless, let each one of you in particular so love his own wife as himself, and let the wife see that she respects her husband."

1 Corinthians 7:14 - NKJ "For the unbelieving husband is sanctified by the wife, and the unbelieving wife is sanctified by the husband, otherwise your children would be unclean, but now they are holy."

A husband in sin is unbelieving, and he will be sanctified (made holy, purified, and blameless) and brought into or back to the Kingdom of God. As you are obedient to the Word of

God, you set yourself in proper position for God to work. As you allow God to sanctify you, the sanctification process begins also in your husband.

It is important to understand that the most important relationship in your live, after your relationship with God, has to be the relationship you have with your husband. If trouble stirs up in your home, you are to go to God. The Holy Spirit is the greatest counselor available. Do not look to mom, dad, sister, brother, aunt, uncle, neighbors, friends, etc. If a third party is needed, seek godly counsel from your church.

You need to examine yourself and see just how you spend your time. Is your friend of choice your husband, or are other friends more important than him? A real pitfall to marriage can be families. After marriage some women want to spend all of their time with siblings or mom and dad. This is not good and it is not God! Marriage, God's divine institution, was meant to be a sanctuary in which a man and a woman would find fulfillment. All of this may scare you, but God will help you to turn your mess into a miracle. I told God, "I don't want my marriage fixed, I want a brand new marriage that is full of the resurrection life of Christ." Believe God to give you a glorious new marriage.

When we go back to Adam we see that God knew Adam needed a helpmeet. God gave him woman. Because divorce is not the heart of God he caused Adam and Eve to be united for life.

God was so serious about this that He said, "They shall become one flesh." He took woman out of man, spoke into her who she was to be, then he placed the full-grown woman back into the side of man and spoke over the two of them, that they were one flesh, inseparable.

If your husband is not aligned correctly with God, and you feel you cannot trust him, cannot trust his decisions and are losing hope, hold on to God. Don't give up. You may think, "How can he change? He has his own free will?" You can begin to pray with love and in faith, with proper motives, knowing that God wants this changed even more than you do. You need to keep in mind that divorce is an abomination to God. The Scriptures tell us that God is not willing that any should perish. God is able to release pressure and influence, through your prayers, that will be powerful magnets drawing your mate unto Himself (God). This concept applies to your children as well. The pressure of God makes it ultimately easier for them to say, "Yes Jesus", than to continue in their rebellion. The pressure and persuasiveness of the Holy Spirit can become so strong that your mate really has to actually battle to oppose God. Amazing isn't it! Through your prayers you make rebellion the hardest possible thing for your mate to do. God never violates their free will, but your intercession brings the most powerful pressure in the universe upon them.

P R   *Lord give me a simple and unselfish desire to be led by my husband as I am led by you, and thereby bring glory to your name. Amen.*

A Y E R   *God it's just you and me. I trust your power to enable me to respond to my husband with love, when you and I know this will be the hardest thing I will ever have to do. I am relying on your promises and trusting in you. As I am faithful to apply your concepts, you will work out the anger and hostility that tears at our home. Amen.*

Father, I thank you that I can trust you through

this situation to make me more like Jesus. I know that you love me even more than I love myself, and that you are vitally concerned with our marriage. I trust you to use these tragic circumstances to draw us both closer to Christ and to teach us valuable lessons we may not have learned any other way. I know that if I learn and apply your concepts to our marriage, you will work in and through both of us to reunite us, rekindle the love we once had, and restore the home we so dearly love, in Jesus' name. Amen.

6

A helpmeet,
Not a Hindrance

Genesis 2:18 - NKJ "And the Lord said, 'it is not good that man should be alone; I will make him a helper, comparable to him.'"

KJV "And the Lord God said, 'it is not good that the man should be alone; I will make him an help meet for him.'"

• Helpmeet means counterpart, one correspondent to himself, companion, suitable helper who will complete him, partner, a mate of his own kind, to aid, to help, to surround, to protect

Proverbs 14:1 - NKJ "The wise woman builds her house. But the foolish woman tears it down with her hands."

• Hindrance the state of being hindered.

• Hinder - To do harm, to impair, to damage, to hamper. To make slow or difficult the course or progress of. To keep from occurring, starting, or continuing; to hold back or prevent.

God uses us to work out His perfect plan for marriage. If we are hindering God's plan in any way, we are in rebellion. Nearly every day in our marriages we have the opportunity to rebel. In the big and little, everyday situations, there is a "God way" to handle it and a "flesh way." You must choose, in every situation, to lay aside all rebellion, and to flow in obedience to God and His Word, because of your love for Him and also your fear of Him.

The Bible says, "The fear of God is the beginning of all wisdom." Once He shows us a truth in His Word, such as a woman is to be her husband's helpmeet, He expects us to be obedient to that Word. Not to do so is simply rebellion against God. We should tremble at the thought of rebelling against God. Take a moment and examine your heart. Do you have genuine "fear of God"? If you answer no, then spend time before God and ask Him to change your heart. This is imperative for you to walk in the level of truth that God desires.

Choose today to be the wise woman that builds her house by applying the Word of God to her life and situations, and allows God to change her heart to agree with the heart of God. By hindering your husband you interfere with God's plan and cause your husband not to hear from God and be changed. Our God is an awesome God; he does not need our help. The best thing we can do is obey and get out of His way and let Him do His perfect will in our marriages.

As we look at the definition of "helpmeet" we see that a woman is to aid, to help, to surround, to protect, be a companion and a counterpart. From these definitions, we see that a woman is to complete her husband. Also, we see that a woman is very important to her husband. As she becomes his helpmeet, she helps to make him "look good". She helps him to be "honored in the city gates". As he is respected and blessed, she is respected and blessed. And a husband will be blessed as his wife is "honored in the city gates". When a woman responds in her marriage according to God's Word, it is a win-win situation for both she and her husband.

Looking again at hindrance, we see a wife who hinders causes harm, damage, hampers and impairs her husband. Some women have fallen into a pattern of making things difficult for their husbands. They put up roadblocks to prevent the very things that they may be praying for. If you fit into the definition of "one who hinders", even if it is in a small way, cry out to God to deliver you. Remember, as you cooperate with your husband and become his helpmeet, your entire family is blessed. When you become a hindrance to him, the entire family suffers.

Let's continue discovering more about being a helpmeet. I want to note here that I didn't get a full revelation of this right away. I felt, as I changed, that I was doing right things. I didn't truly understand that I needed to study my husband and find out what he needed for a helpmeet. Study your husband. Ask God to show you what he needs. This can be a very exciting time for you and your husband. Trust me, your marriage will be revitalized.

Notice, God did not give a command for women to do specific things to be helpers for their husbands. Every marriage is different. What your husband needs from you is different from what Richard needs from me. We must know our husbands intimately. I'm not talking about sex. I'm talking about how they feel, think, and respond. A huge problem today is work and outside activities leave little time to cultivate the depth of relationship God wants in our marriages. Don't let this happen to you. Make sure you leave time to know your husband, make it a priority. We are to be correspondent to him (fitting and conforming). If we are to complete our husbands, doesn't it stand to reason that we must know him deeply?

When we look at our "to do" list from God, it is clear we have enough on our plates to keep us busy for the rest of our lives. However, if we do it with the right attitude it becomes a labor of love. We greatly benefit from it and so do our husbands. We all know God doesn't want idle women running around to and fro without a purpose. He wants us to actively participate in completing His perfect will for our lives and marriages.

Next we'll look at the word counterpart. The dictionary defines counterpart as one of two corresponding copies of a legal instrument (duplicate); fitting something perfectly; complement (something that fills up, completes or makes perfect); one remarkably similar to another; one having the same function or characteristic as another.

Sound impossible? All things are possible with God. If you are like most women I know, you look at your husband and say, "we are exact opposites." Well God knew that, He decided to find someone for you and for me who was just the opposite, so the things missing in you and me are found in him. Your husband is a gem, but maybe you have not done enough digging yet to find that precious treasure.

As our husband's counterpart, we fit together to make each other complete; we compliment, fill up, and make each other perfect. As we allow God to change us, we begin to find we are becoming remarkably similar to one another. We find out we are on the same team and not in competition and playing against each other. Then, when God gets His hands on our mates and begins a corresponding work in them, we become one (two corresponding copies of a legal instrument called marriage - duplicates).

Now is the time to take inventory of your marriage. Test yourself on the following questions:

♦ Do you compliment your husband?

♦ Do you always try to fill him up and do everything you can to help him become perfected?

♦ Do you build him up with your mouth and your actions?

♦ When out in public do you have to correct everything he says, or can you just let some things go by even when you know that you are right?

Do you have similar desires as your husband, or do you put pressure on him to live in a bigger house than you can afford; buy clothes, furnishings, etc. that you can't afford; go on vacations you can't afford; socialize constantly when he's exhausted, etc.? In the natural, as you look at you and your husband, do you feel that you two fit? Ask God to put on your heart what additional questions you should ask.

You can see the danger when a woman does not have agreement with her husband and begins making financial demands they cannot afford. I have observed over the last fourteen years, women placing unrealistic demands on their husbands. These men have to meet these demands or pay the price of an unhappy wife. I've seen men get into financial ruin to stop a nagging wife. This is not God's plan. Do not press your husband beyond your means. I've seen women press their husbands so far into debt, that they were forced to work themselves, and then resented their husbands for not providing. Understand that when he says no

to something, it is for good reason. If it's not for good reason, or if he is stingy and unreasonably withholding from you, then pray for God to change his heart.

I want to give you a little detail on part of my testimony in chapter one. I mentioned earlier that we lived in Michigan, in a very nice neighborhood in an adequate ranch house. My husband had a decent position with his company, but with four small children we were just making it financially.

One-by-one the people we were closest to, began to move into larger houses in nicer neighborhoods. No longer was I satisfied with my ranch house. After visiting a friend who lived in a lovely area, I decided we just had to have a larger house. And wouldn't you know it, we found the perfect house. The inside of the house perfectly matched everything we owned. That could sound like God, couldn't it? It had a gorgeous yard with many trees. The neighborhood was wonderful and the families that lived there seemed just like us. On the outside everything look great. So we bought it.

Our children thrived there and we made wonderful friends. I loved it there because I was a social being and we had a wonderful social life. Everyone had children the same ages and we got along great together. The problem was, the people there had twice the income of my husband. It was getting harder and harder to manage our finances. We were constantly taking from one area to pay another. Finally, we realized there was no real future for my husband at his company, and we just weren't making it financially, so he took a position with a new company that was starting in Pittsburgh.

Our house didn't sell right away and I stayed in Michigan while Richard worked in Pittsburgh until our children had to start school. We built a beautiful new home in Pittsburgh. I've always been blessed with beautiful homes. The day we left Michigan was one of the saddest in my life. It felt like we were leaving family behind, and I knew that since they were not really family, we would eventually lose contact, which we have.

A short while after we were in Pittsburgh, Richard said, "I'll never let you do to me again what you did to me in Michigan. I'll never let you talk me into moving into a house we can't afford. We had to leave Michigan because you were not satisfied with the house we had. You had to have a big house like all your friends." He also said, "Never will I allow myself to be talked into social activity like we had in Michigan. I couldn't stand it."

When I head this, I was in shock, but I listened. Which for that period in our lives was a miracle. I didn't listen to a whole lot of what he said. I felt I had all the answers. This was the beginning of God grabbing hold of my heart. For as I thought about it, I realized he was right. My demands forced us to leave the place we so loved. I also know that God covered us when we left Michigan, because from Pittsburgh we went to Ohio and then from Ohio to Indiana. It was in Indiana that Richard and I met the Lord after twenty-five years of marriage; and then our real life finally began. Who knows what would have happened to us if we stayed in Michigan.

So I understand from first-hand experience what it means to cause your husband to meet your wishes even though he hates doing it. This just caused more resentment to build up in him. By my usurping his authority, God allowed me to experience a devastating loss. This happened in 1975 and I can remember it just like it happened yesterday. There are some things God doesn't want us to forget.

As a helpmeet you are to keep an open eye and a listening third ear to everything your husband says and does, with the internal intention to help him and be a part of everything he is doing. This does not mean you jump in and take control. But that you are willing to come along side and help in any and all areas where he may need you.

How many of us have actually been this kind of suitable helper to our husbands? If we answer honestly, I don't think many would be able to answer yes. Granted, we might not always have the ability to be a suitable helper. If our heart is to be this helper, our husbands will understand when we can't.

Human beings are innately selfish. We must set aside this selfishness and live our lives according to the Word and God's perfect plan. Don't demand your own time, your own space, and your own things. Be a suitable helper even if your plate is full at the moment. Help even if you feel it is something you don't see as worthwhile. Stay attached; stay involved, live as one flesh as the Bible commands.

Understanding and living out your correct position with your husband is critical for a good, strong God centered marriage. The Word tells us a house divided can't stand.

Mark 3:25 - NKJ "And if a house is divided against itself, that house cannot stand."

Take time to pray now and ask the Holy Spirit, your teacher, to help you become the helpmeet that your husband needs.

P
R
A
Y
E
R

Lord without you I am helpless and hopeless, but I can do all things through you Jesus, who strengthens me. Thank you Holy Spirit for teaching me how to be a helpmeet to my "OWN" husband. Thank you for comforting me and enabling me to carry out this task. Do not allow me to take this lightly, as this is really important to you and it's really vital for our marriage to become all that you desire it to be. God keep me from causing division in my marriage. I do not want to be a foolish woman and tear down my marriage with my own hands, but I want to be a wise women who will build my home wisely according to your Word. Thank you Lord that you can help me change. Thank you that as I am obedient to You and to your Word, You will change me. I give you, in advance, all the glory for the change. I praise and glorify you now, in the name of Jesus. AMEN!

7

How Can I be
My Husband's Companion?

Next let's look at companion.

+ Companion - One that accompanies another, one
  that is closely connected to something similar,
  associate, to keep company with, being sociable.

Over the years I've had to really examine and assess
myself honestly. When it was convenient for me I
was a good companion to my husband. I always did
the functional things when we went out to dinner or church
or had pre-planned activities with the children.

God showed me I really wasn't a "good companion"
because I only wanted to be a companion on my terms.
Sometimes when I was in the midst of a project or working
around the house and my husband wanted to go do some
running around outside of our home, I wasn't willing to drop
everything and go. If he would ask me to go, I would go, but
I wouldn't voluntarily drop everything and go on my own.

We are all selfish and see our own things as important.
I'm not saying that you have to always do everything together
and can never have separate time. As women we need to
examine our hearts and look at the priorities in our lives.

Our first priority must be our relationship with God. Then next should come our relationship with our husband, then our children, etc.

When new couples are dating they can't wait to be together. Companionship is uppermost in their minds. They figure out things to do and plan ways to spend more time together. If a girl's busy and her guy calls, she drops everything for him and goes off with him. Then comes marriage, and suddenly your busy with work, hobbies, family, friends, television, and everything else life throws you way. Amazingly, it is no longer "cool" to hang out with each other like you used to.

Children come along and mom gets so busy she can hardly squeeze time in for dad. Suddenly, they realize that they barely spend any time together. They have good intentions to spend more time together, but days, weeks, months and sometimes years pass by and they never remedy their situation. The children get older, become involved in more activities and suddenly they find that they have even less time.

Husbands and wives begin to become short and irritated with each other. There is very little if any personal satisfaction in their relationship and they begin to look elsewhere for emotional fulfillment.

A husband and wife are to receive their emotional fulfillment from each other. If a couple is not fulfilled emotionally, physically, and spiritually with each other, they will turn elsewhere for this fulfillment. Many a marriage has broken up because spouses quit being each other's companion and someone else comes in and fills that position.

It is a proven fact that most of the time when there is an extra-marital affair, it's not for looks or for money, but for emotional fulfillment. The man who seems to never talk at home finds a "Chatty Kathy" at work, at the restaurant, at his favorite store, etc. who is so interested in him and what he has to say. Soon he finds himself seeking out the one who is interested in him. The more time spent in this environment, the more opportunity to fall. I am not saying that this is correct, for everyone should be able to control his own emotions and feelings. What I am trying to bring out here is that every man should have this need met in his own home, by his own wife. Maybe the man did not go so far as to have an extra-marital affair, but committed adultery in his heart.

If this emotional intimacy has been broken in your marriage, you must believe God will rekindle it. It may not look like there is any hope of rebuilding the fire, but the glorious news is God wants to blow on your fire and ignite the embers that He's kept alive even though you can't see or feel them.

It used to be that men were more likely to have extra-marital affairs, but statistics are showing that more and more women are having extra-marital affairs — and for the same reasons as men. Their husbands do not support them emotionally. Their husbands are too busy to spend time with them. Maybe he just doesn't know how to get into her life, or how to let her into his. This is a modern-day crisis in marriage. When a woman spends her time looking at soap operas and other television programs that depict fast-paced, exciting, and sensual lives, takes a look at her life, she begins to hate it. Or, it happens to the woman whose male co-worker is interested in every aspect of her life. She begins to think, "I'm really missing it with this guy I'm married to". Then the same scenario takes place with her as with the man. If she's not committing actual adultery, she begins to commit emotional adultery.

God had a perfect plan when He gave Adam, woman for his companion. She was to be his emotional support, his companion, his lover, and his completion. God wants this in all our marriages. The glorious news is that He so wants this, that if you are willing, He will do a work in your marriage that will astound you. He did it for me. What God has done in my life, in my marriage, is so glorious. He performed multi-miracles in our lives. He took us from the brink of divorce, to ecstasy, from virtually no communication, to total communication, from nothing in common, to everything in common, from complete separation, to a co-habitation of oneness. But as mentioned earlier, this took place because I was willing to change. He worked on me one area at a time, one day at a time.

Are you willing to change? If you say yes, God will more than meet you. A little add-on here, as I was obedient to the things God showed me, and kept my mouth and my eyes and my actions off of my husband, he sought God for change in his life. I believe God initiated this desire in my husband's life, because originally he felt he didn't need to change anything. Isn't God good!

Lack of companionship does not always have such devastating results such as physical or emotional adultery. Many times a friend, a neighbor or family members will come and take over the spare time a woman has. If you are not careful, all your time can be stolen from you by phone calls, visits, and unnecessary demands on your time. Family and friends and neighbors are wonderful and everyone needs these relationships. The danger comes when you allow these relationships to interfere with your home and family life. When your husband comes home from work or wherever else, your full attention should go to him. You shouldn't be thinking "oh no, he's home already".

You may look at your marriage and say, "this has gotten so far away from God's plan, help me bring it back." The first thing you have to remember is that God is in this with you. He is looking for your heart to be right. Man may look at the outward appearance, but God looks at your heart. Ask God to change your heart. Ask Him to give you the desire to be your husband's companion.

A companion is, in all reality, a friend. A friend sticks close by another and walks with another. Companions can frequently be together and not even talk. They just like being in the same place close together. They receive great comfort just looking up and knowing the other one is there. You and your husband can be in the same room, both doing separate things, but being joined in the spirit by just being together. This is the way God wants it; love, peace, joy, unity, bonding at all times, whether talking or silent, busy or resting, walking or driving.

We all need to cultivate friendship in our marriages. If you feel that things are not the way they should be, or if you feel there is great animosity between you and your husband, then you need a game plan for change. Remember the definition for insanity is, "to continue to do the same thing and expect different results or change".

When we meet someone and feel we would like them for a friend, what are some of the things we might do? First of all, we would make sure that we speak in a welcoming manner, kindly, with respect and with our entire manner showing that we acknowledge them. We would extend ourselves to this person, finding out the things they like. Next we would be hospitable and serve them in a special manner. We would make ourselves available, if at all possible, when they wanted to do something. Then we would surely extend kindness and invitations to show them we are interested in pursuing this friendship. As time would go by we would surely, if we wanted to be a true friend, try to find out what they like to do and accommodate them and not just think of ourselves. Get the picture? What are some things you would do if you desired to make your husband your friend?

Maybe you never had a close friend. Then ask the Holy Spirit to teach you and guide you step-by-step into developing friendship with your mate. You may say, "He doesn't want to be my friend". And that may be a true at this moment, but with God all things are possible. Trust God, maybe in a way that you have never trusted Him before. Reach out and take God's hand and let Him lead you through this.

P R A Y E R

Dear Lord, our lacking friendship and companionship seems like an insurmountable obstacle in our lives. I know that I cannot do this by myself, but through You, I can do all things. God, I want to release my marriage to you. I desire change. Change me, Oh Lord. I present myself to you and say, "here I am, change me". In fact, I cry out to you, oh Lord, 'CHANGE ME'! I will not look at what my husband is doing or what the results of my actions are. My desire is to be obedient to you. I will develop this friendship as unto you. I know that to develop this relationship will take time. I pledge to you to be patient. I will not be weary in well doing, for in due season, I will reap my harvest, because Your Word says so. My goal is to be your obedient daughter. I so want to be obedient, that no matter what the outcome, I'll be obedient to You and Your Word. Thank you Lord for your great love and concern for me. Amen.

8

Submission is the Key to "One-Flesh"

God has a glorious plan for every marriage. That plan is the union of "oneness", whereby two come together and actually become "one flesh". Woman was taken out of the side of man and built up into her full beauty. When she marries, God puts her back into the side of the man so that she can mature into her "God-ordained", beauty of "completion".

From experience I can tell you that there is no greater place than the place of "oneness" or "one flesh". There is such love, contentment, peace, joy, companionship, and fulfillment in this place. But there is a door that a woman must walk through before she and her husband will come into that place of being truly "one". That door is the door of submission. To many women the word submission is a very nasty word. It conjures up images of being a doormat, of having no rights, or of being a nothing in their marriage. None of this is true. We are going to look into godly submission, not what the world would call submission.

Let's look at the scenario being played out in millions of homes today. The women's liberation groups have been active in "setting women free" during the past 40 plus years. Women needed to "do their own thing". They needed to get away from "male dominated rule". Their bodies were their own and nobody was going to tell them what they could or could not do. And there should be no separation or definition of gender.

What has all of this accomplished for women? Today, the bond of marriage is no longer sacred and divorce is rampant. Couples divorce over simple issues. This has left our country with an epidemic of single mothers. The majority of them cannot earn enough income to properly care for their families. Many times they have to go on welfare. The largest poverty group in our country now is "single mothers". Somehow this change does not appear to me to be a change that set women free.

Then as they got away from "male dominated rule", they began to have trouble holding down jobs, trouble submitting to any authorities in their lives, trouble having relationships with males and certainly trouble with their husbands. As things began to fall down around them, (and surely they would fall with this kind of an attitude), great bitterness would enter their hearts and they would feel that they could trust no one. You look around today and many women who were part of this movement have matured into disappointed and bitter women. Freedom? I don't think so.

We all know of the tragedy of abortion. " No one has the right to tell someone what they can do with their own body". The argument goes on and on. Through our post-abortion ministry, I personally have ministered to hundreds and hundreds of women, who in their youth, bought the lie that their bodies were their own and aborted their babies.

When a woman has had an abortion the time will come when she must come to terms with the fact that she is living in bondage, fear, regret, poverty of spirit and sometimes poverty of the womb. She must resolve that she did not experience freedom through her abortion but received instead a prison of her own regret. Fortunately, through the love and grace of

God, and through repentance, all of this can be healed. God is so good to care about our past mistakes.

Did the women's liberation movement bring freedom to women? No, it brought tragedy. Women are experiencing an epidemic of sexually transmitted diseases. If not an epidemic, there are many women who are sterile and not able to have children when they so desperately want to. I could give more examples, but I think you see the picture.

Now look at the issue of no separation between genders and no definition of gender. God said, "Male and female I created them". So what do we have now? We have open blatant lesbianism. We see it on television. You can even go into beauty shops and look at magazines and see two women in compromising embraces and know that they are trying to show more than friendship. Basically, the media is trying to brainwash young girls. Our young people are so confused. They no longer have strong gender identification. They are struggling with their purpose and destiny in life. Women and young girls are so hard, so insensitive. Their very actions are emasculating their fathers, husbands, brothers, boyfriends, friends, and all males around them. Many of these girls find themselves lonely and isolated. They never truly find fulfillment in life. Now as we look at this group, would we say that they are free? No they are bound by their own confusion and their own actions.

Young women bring this confusion into their marriages. This produces warped expectations of the roles of a husband and wife. Women demanding equality, and expecting their husbands to treat them as "one of the guys" one minute and then as their wives the next, often don't want it once they experience all that it entails.

This is all such a tragedy that one could begin to feel hopeless, but God. Don't you love that phrase, but God?

God has a plan for all women. For children to be submitted to their parents, women to be submitted to their husbands, and husbands to be submitted to God.

> Ephesians 6:1-3 - AMP "Children, obey your parents in the Lord (as His representatives), for this is just and right. Honor (esteem and value as precious) your father and your mother—this is the first commandment with a promise—that all may be well with you and that you may live long on the earth."

As women we are to be submitted to all the governing authorities.

> Romans 13:1-3 - AMP "Let every person be loyally subject to the governing (civil) authorities. For there is no authority except from God (by His permission, His sanction), and those that exist do so by God's appointment. Therefore he who resists and sets himself up against the authorities resists what God has appointed and arranged (in divine order). And those who resist will bring down judgment upon themselves (receiving the penalty due them). For civil authorities are not a terror to (people of) good conduct, but to (those of) bad behavior. Would you have no dread of him who is in authority? Then do what is right and you will receive his approval and commendation."

I love what it says in this scripture, if we're doing what we're supposed to be doing there's no fear of the policeman stopping us or the tax collector coming to the door or the sheriff arresting us for domestic disturbances. No, we love the authorities, for we know that they are in place to help

enhance our lives, (usually). We also know there may be some elected authorities we do not agree with. Those we are to pray for.

We are to submit to employment authorities, store authorities, school authorities, etc. God has gone into detail in His Word to show us there is an authority structure in place and we are to submit to it.

> 1 Peter 2:13 - AMP "Be submissive to every human institution and authority for the sake of the Lord, whether it be to the emperor as supreme."

God places spiritual authorities in our lives and expects us to honor and respect those authorities. The exception to all of this is when an authority requests us to be disobedient to the Word of God. The Word of God is a higher authority than these that I am mentioning here. A wonderful rule of thumb for spiritual authorities is look at their fruit. (I use the word "fruit" to mean the results someone's life or ministry is producing.) Fruit or lack of it in one's life, will be able to tell you so much about an individual.

> Hebrews 13:7 - AMP "Remember your leaders and superiors in authority (for it was they) who brought to you the Word of God. Observe attentively and consider their manner of living (the outcome of their well-spent lives) and imitate their faith (their conviction that God exists and is the Creator and Ruler of all things, the Provider and Bestower of eternal salvation through Christ, and their leaning of the entire human personality on God in absolute trust and confidence in His power, wisdom and goodness.)"

After looking at all of this we understand that God is very interested in us having correct authority in every area of our lives. Would it not make sense that He would have an authority structure in marriage? We've already seen that He has one regarding the children. One of the definitions of authority in the dictionary is "delegated power over others". I love that. God has given our husbands through marriage, delegated power or authority over us. Why has he done this? Because He loves us! Someone has to be in charge. In my husband's business the rule is "when two people are in charge, no one is in charge".

Another definition of authority is "the right to make final decisions". That's exactly what God wants in marriage. He wants the wife to have total input in every area, with the understanding that her husband has the right to make the final decision.

Also the dictionary says, "One in authority carries with their position the ability to receive submission". This is the way it is in marriage. A husband, by the very nature of his role, carries with that role the ability (given by God) to receive submission from his wife. With God it doesn't stop there. The goal of godly submission is not someone giving orders and another one bowing down under those orders. Godly submission is a wife willingly submitting because she knows that God's plan is the best plan. The goal is proper alignment, so the man can function completely and freely in his role and love his wife unconditionally, and become truly "one flesh" with her. This is impossible when a husband and wife are in competition for headship. When two people are competing you have division, no leader, and certainly no oneness.

Let's look at the Word of God regarding submission in marriage. We have to keep in mind we are to be doers of the Word and not just hearers. God's Word is a manual for our lives. Before Jesus, I floundered in my marriage, after Jesus I had an anchor to cling to — Jesus; a map to guide me — the Word of God; and a captain to guide me — the Holy Spirit. Isn't the very thought of all of that "AWESOME"!!

God's Divine Plan

Ephesians 5:21-33 - AMP "Be subject to one another out of reverence for Christ (the Messiah, the Anointed One). Wives, be subject (be submissive and adapt yourselves) to your own husbands as (a service) to the Lord. For the husband is the head of the wife as Christ is the Head of the church, Himself the Savior of (His) body. As the church is subject to Christ, so let wives also be subject in everything to their husbands.

Husbands, love your wives, as Christ loved the church and gave Himself up for her, so that He might sanctify her, having cleansed her by the washing of water with the Word, that He might present the church to Himself in glorious splendor, without spot or wrinkle or any such thing (that she might be holy and faultless). Even so husbands should love their wives as (being in a sense) their own bodies. He who loves his own wife loves himself. For no man ever hated his own flesh, but nourishes and carefully protects and cherishes it, as Christ does the church, because we are members (parts) of His body.

For this reason a man shall leave his father and his mother and shall be joined to his wife, and the two shall become one flesh. This mystery is very great, but I speak concerning (the relation of) Christ and the church.

However, let each man of you (without exception) love his wife as (being in a sense) his very own self; and let the wife see that she respects and reverences her husband (that she notices him, regards him, honors him, prefers him, venerates, and esteems him; and that she defers to him, praises him, and loves and admires him exceedingly)."

Our goal is still to be a doer of the Word, not just a hearer of the Word. Isn't God wonderful to give us His glorious Word in such detail to teach and to train us? (I marvel at the fact that before the foundation of the world, God cared about this very moment in time, so that multitudes of women could be helped.) The scripture tells us to be subject or submissive to each other (husband and wife). Through this we understand that instructions are forthcoming to both regarding their role in marriage. This is to be done out of reverence (or honor or obedience) for Christ who is our Anointed One. His Anointing will enable us to do all that we need to do.

It goes on to say, that as wives we are to be subject to and adapt ourselves to our own husbands as a service to the Lord. So God is asking us to do this as a service to Him. That really puts a different slant on this, doesn't it? To me it says, "if I love God, and want to serve Him, and want to be obedient to God, and if I understand that I need to have a holy fear of God, then being submissive and adapting to my husband (not your husband, but my husband), is not an impossibility, nor should it be difficult. Really, it takes putting God's desires and your husband's desires above your desires.

For women who have been in charge and in control in their marriage this will require some adjustment. Understand that this is God's plan for you, and purpose in your heart to be obedient to God and His plan. Now that this Word has been revealed to you, you are required to be obedient to it. You will have to die to self in regards to running things and ask your husband how he would like things done.

Take this step-by-step. Submission is not a teaching you learn today and perfect in your life by the end of the week. God will show you, day-by-day, in each and every facet of your marriage, how to correctly submit to your husband. As this happens, your husband begins to submit also, and the end result is oneness.

This will take time. Be patient. God will meet you where you are. God has placed inside each of us a desire to be who "He says we are". Granted, you might not be functioning correctly in your God-given role, but God knows that. He made provision for help though the Holy Spirit and His Word. Submit to His authority by submitting to your husband.

In working with couples I have found that when a woman goes to her husband and asks him for forgiveness for not allowing him to be the head of the family he is greatly re-lieved. Do you need to ask your husband to forgive you for not allowing him to be the head of the family? If you do then don't delay. It will be a great relief for both of you and a blessing in your marriage.

Submission is an act of your will. Get under your husband's leadership in the family with the knowledge that it's God's will for you. Your husband cannot lead your family if you are not willing to follow, or worse, trying to lead him. Submission is, first of all, an act of obedience to God. Then, with the grace of God flowing through your body, soul and spirit, you can submit to your husband. When you do this according to God's design, it's easy. God will cause all of us to be obedient one way or another, when we rebel then it becomes hard and unpleasant. Today, make a choice to do it God's way. Let your teacher, the Holy Spirit, guide you and lead you every step of the way. He can, you know. If you're ready for the transformation to begin, please pray the following prayer.

P
R
A
Y
E
R

Dear Lord, this is a big step for me, because I have no idea what lies ahead. It's taken me a long time just to get where I am now and you are asking me to change everything. But today, I choose to trust you; I choose to show my love and reverence for you through my obedience to you. I want to change, so I pray change me. Father today I turn in my pants. I no longer want to wear the pants in the family. Forgive me for being an independent wife. Forgive me for controlling my husband. Forgive me for keeping such a tight grip on everything and not trusting, first of all, you and then my husband. (If applicable) Forgive my mother and father for setting a wrong example of headship for me. Forgive me for showing our children a wrong example of headship. Father, I place the Blood of Jesus over all of my sin and ask you to wash it white as snow. Father, thank you for grace. I go to your mountain of grace and I appropriate all I need for the task ahead.

Today, I bind the spirits of independence, rebellion and control and break their power over my life and my family's life. I shut the door to them generationally. I ask you to cleanse all the defilement out of our family that is a result of these spirits. I break the power of all curses brought about because of this over our family. Father loose into our family a spirit of submission and then a spirit of obedience to you. Father release unto our family generational blessings. Show me Lord, how to be submissive to my own husband. Help us Lord to become one. I will not look at my husband but only at myself. It is not my business what you are doing with him. That is your business. Help me to die in every area that is necessary. Thank you Father, that step-by-step, you are changing me. I trust you. I cry out for joy to well up in my heart as I am obedient to you. I bless you and thank you in the name of Jesus. Amen

9

Adapt to Him and His Plans

Y̶ou may read the chapter title and think, "but wait, what about my plans". God does not require a woman to go into servitude in her marriage. He does not forbid her to make a plan, have mind of her own, nor be a contributor in decisions. But we all know, at times, we do not agree on everything. That is the time when you must let go and fit into your husband's plans or decisions. Our goal in marriage is for "oneness". When you reach an impasse in your decision process, someone's idea has to die. In order that the home function correctly and that peace remain at all times, God made provision for this in His Word.

> 1 Peter 3:1 - AMP "In like manner, you married women, be submissive to your own husbands, (subordinate yourselves as being secondary to and dependent on them, and ADAPT yourselves to them), so that even if any do not obey the Word of God, they may be won over not by discussion, but by the godly lives of their wives."

We see that as you submit and adapt to your husband's authority, God has an inroad to him, to begin to turn him and change him. Many times you know that what you're feeling is correct, but your husband will not see it your way. Let go. Submit to him and adapt to him. At the same time release it to God, saying "Lord, Your will be done on earth as it is in Heaven in this situation". Many times God will intervene and change your husband's mind. Should he not change his mind and go ahead with a wrong decision, if you keep quiet, God can work through that mistake to change him.

In today's society, women have their own plans. They like it that way. Years ago it was easier for a woman to fit into her husband's plans, because with one car, no outside employment, limited money, and no television, women anxiously waited for their husbands to return home so they could be together. Today, instead of women waiting with their noses at the windowpane for their husbands to come and spend time with the family, the attitude is "Oh you're home already". I have some plans tonight. Your dinner is in the refrigerator, just heat it up in the microwave." And off they go. That is an example of what adapting isn't. Even though there may be times when this scenario has to play out at your house, it should not be the norm.

God put you two together as husband and wife, till death do you part. Find a way to spend quality time together. As a rule, a great deal of a man's time is taken up with his work and spiritual commitment, so God asks the woman to be sensitive to this and adapt to her husband. The reward for doing this will be great. If you don't know how to do this, ask your teacher, the Holy Spirit. Commit in your heart to be a doer of the Word. Lets look at what the word adapt means.

- Adapt means to make suitable or fit, as for a particular purpose or situation.
To adjust oneself to particular conditions or ways - To bring oneself into harmony with a particular environment - To bring one's self, one's acts, one's behavior or mental state into

harmony with changed conditions or your environment - A suiting or fitting alteration or modification.

Synonyms for adapt are adjust, accommodate, conform, reconcile

*   Accommodate is to furnish with something desired, needed or suited.

*   Conform is to shape, to fit or make like
    To bring into or be in harmony or agreement with

*   Conformed is to be jointly formed, similar, conformed to, fashioned like unto

*   Reconcile is to restore to compatibility or harmony - To change

*   Adjust is to bring into a more satisfactory state. To put into order - To achieve harmonious and mental behavioral balance between one's own personal needs and striving and the demands of other individuals

So we go back to the beginning in Genesis, where God took woman out of man, and now in marriage, puts woman back into the side of man, and she becomes formed to her husband, similar to her husband, conformed to her husband and fashioned like unto him as "one". Why? Because God says they are one - "one flesh". If you're struggling with adapting, lay down your struggling now, and do this God's way. It is so wonderful. Richard and I have been married almost 40 years now. We didn't learn any of this until we were married for 25 years. Just think if we had started out from the beginning in the truth of God's Word. Wherever you are now, put your stake in the ground and commit to change; do it God's way.

You have to sow into your marriage to have a harvest. Adapting is a key element for a bonded, lasting marriage. We all want a lasting fulfilled relationship with our mate. Even if you are now saying in your heart, "No I don't. You don't know how rotten he treats me. I can't. I can't." You may not realize it, but deep down inside you is sparking a ray of hope. "If this were only true. If it would only work for me." All I can say is just try it. Remember the slogan "TRY GOD"!

> Galatians 6:7-9 - AMP "Do not be deceived, God is not mocked, for whatever a man sows, that he will also reap. For he who sows to his flesh will of the flesh reap corruption, but he who sows to the Spirit will of the Spirit reap everlasting life and let us not grow weary in well doing for in due season you shall reap if you don't grow weary."

The Lord has spelled out in His Word the need, (yes the need, so that completion can take place), for a wife to submit to her husband's headship. We need to do this willingly and with joy. A home in order brings great blessing for the entire family. A home out of order will bring chaos, disaster, and curses. Adapting is a slightly different twist on submission. Submission is conforming to a request of your husband or letting go when you disagree. Adapting is doing the things God shows you to do before your husband asks. Knowing him so well that you adapt and change in anticipation of what he desires. This will bring you and your husband into greater "oneness". Once again, our teacher, the Holy Spirit is at work. How wonderful is the work of the Holy Spirit!

Finances are a key you need to adapt to. When you married your husband, you married his financial potential. If you were raised in a home where you were indulged, but now your husband can only afford a modest lifestyle, then adapt to his income and the standard of living he can afford.

Many women go to work because they want a nicer home, nicer furniture, nicer car, nicer clothes, etc. You and your family will be cheated if you work long hours and have little time and energy left, just to provide a higher standard of living. The following story gives an illustration of what I am referring to.

When they got married the woman had a degree and the potential of earning a higher income than her husband. They based their budget, including buying a home, cars, etc. on their joint income, of which she was the major breadwinner. After they were married for a while they wanted a family. She, especially, wants a baby. God has put that into all women to want a baby. The baby comes and she plans to go right back to work, only to find out she doesn't want to go back to work. She wants to stay home and take care of her baby. This is her baby and she doesn't want strangers taking care of the baby.

It breaks her heart as she leaves the baby behind. The stress of working full time and taking care of the baby, along with the guilt, makes her emotionally sick. She then becomes angry with her husband because he doesn't have a higher earning potential. Don't let this happen to you. The sad thing is she knew this when she married him, but they didn't base their purchases on his income, or at the very most, his income, with minimal help from her.

Even if the woman is not the main breadwinner, but has

a part or full time job, and decides to quit working after the baby arrives, you have to adapt and adjust to fit into the constraints of one income. Many times this means no extras for a few years. Women have to be able to adapt to this and not run up bills, have secret charge accounts, borrow money from loan companies or parents, and then live in fear of how to tell their husbands. These, and many more deceitful things are situations we have dealt with in counseling.

As a married woman, whether you work or don't work is between you, your husband, and God. You are to adapt into your husband's plans. Do not go out and get a job if your husband does not want you to. It will only bring dissension and trouble into your household. It will not be a blessing. The ideal situation is for women to be home and be keepers of their home. But we know that this may not be possible for everyone. If you are working, try to live off of your husband's salary. If the day comes when you have to quit it will not be a hardship for you.

Being a loving wife, taking care of a home, nurturing your husband and children and working can be a strain on a woman. Another important issue to consider when you work is that you have two authorities in your life, your husband and your boss. Your boss may ask you to do something that your husband won't like, such as working overtime. Who will you be loyal to? If your husband insists that you work, then adapt to his desires and work. Just make sure that it's something he wants and not something that you manipulated him into.

Make sure your salary will more than compensate for all of your expenses. You may go to work and end up working for nothing, or worse yet, end up having it cost you money to go to work. Following are some calculations I made:

♦ Part-time job

20 hours per week @ $7/hr	$140

Deductions for taxes etc.	$47
25 hours babysitter @ $3 per hour	$75
Gasoline to and from work	$15
Coffee and coke breaks	$10
Two nights at fast-food restaurants	$25
Total expenses	$172

Without any other expenses such as clothes, car insurance etc., you are $32 in the hole. Even with a no-charge babysitter, you would only net $43 or less. None of this takes in wear and tear on you, your husband, and your children. Many times women use working as an escape, but if you have young children you have not escaped. You have only made your life more difficult and have gained nothing. In reality, much has been lost.

There is so much to be gained from being content in your circumstances. Ask God to help you adapt to your husband's income potential. This may take great sacrifice, but in the end, great will be your reward.

When two people marry, they find out just how different they are. When you're dating you are so cute with each other. Little irritations rise up and each of you think, "no problem, I'll change that when we get married". After marriage, one thing is for sure, neither one is interested in the other one changing them. Remember, we have no power or ability to change another person, but we can cry out for God to change us. The following are just a few areas of potential differences. Remember in His Word, God asked the woman to adjust. We are doers of the Word, right?

You may be a night person and he's a day person. Would God want you to adapt to him and become a day person? When you think of a vacation, you think of the ocean, sun and powder white beaches. He's tired and all he wants to do on his vacation is sit home on his patio. Are you willing to adjust and work this out and compromise? Let God work something out that will be pleasing to both of you.

You love plays and movies, and he loves sporting events. Can you get interested in his sporting events and give him space and grace to develop an interest in your movies and plays? Remember as you sow, so will you reap.

Adapting yourself to your husband will take some time and work, but it will also be well worth the effort. Adapting is a vital key to a successful marriage. When we choose not to be selfish, but to honor and adapt to our husbands, God begins to do such a work in their hearts, that they want to lay down their lives for us. My prayer for you is that you will be obedient to this.

1 Samuel 15:22 - AMP "Has the Lord as great a delight in burnt offerings and sacrifices, as in obeying the voice of the Lord? Behold to obey is better than sacrifice and to hearken than the fat of lambs."

P
R
A
Y
E
R

Dear Holy Spirit, my teacher, please help me to understand how to adapt to my husband. Teach me how to do this your way. Show me areas where I am going my own way, wanting what I want and not considering him. Show me where I need to adapt and then give me the grace to adapt. As I adapt, I understand that I will be sowing into my marriage. As I sow, I expect a wonderful, bountiful harvest. Lord, your plan is beautiful. Teach me how to follow your plan, so I can walk in your blessings. Put within my heart, a burning desire to adapt. Please take all rebellion and selfishness out of me. I am not always right and I do not always have to do things my way. Lord, I desire to walk in peace, in obedience to Your will and Your Word. Thank you for helping me to achieve this, in Jesus' name, I pray. Amen.

10

Sex is Not a Game...
It's a God-Thing

Genesis 1:28 - NKJ "Then God blessed them, and God said to them, be fruitful and multiply; fill the earth and subdue it; have dominion over the fish of the sea, over the birds of the air, and over every living thing that moves on the earth."

Genesis 2:24-25 - NKJ "Therefore a man shall leave his father and mother and be joined to his wife, and they shall become one flesh. And they were both naked, the man and his wife, and were not ashamed."

We see that God created man, (woman, in his rib, was one with him), and then brought forth and built up woman, and then put them back together as one-flesh. We see that they were naked and were not ashamed. We can assume that they enjoyed complete, unhindered sexual freedom. Before sin entered they were ecstatic in their freedom. God told them "be fruitful and multiply". He expected them to multiply and provided an avenue for this. This beautiful avenue God gave them, we call "sex". To them "sex" or whatever they called copulation was a beautiful, tender word. It was a God-Thing.

This was the origination of marriage. The plan was one man and one woman united for life. We know, though, that this plan has not been followed through history, but God would like to begin to make glorious history with us. Today can be a new start on your marriage. You can say, "yes God, I am married to this man, (this applies even if it is not your first marriage), and I am going to stay united to him for life.

Man has dirtied up this God-thing called sex. Much of sex today is portrayed as sensual, provocative, dirty, nasty, and the saddest of all - a weapon to be used between husband and wife.

I recently read the following in a book by Richard Booker, called "The Miracle of the Scarlet Thread". [3]

> "A blood covenant between two parties is the closest, the most enduring, the most solemn and the most sacred of all contracts. It absolutely cannot be broken. When you enter into blood covenant with someone, you promise to give them your life, your love, and your protection forever — till death do you part. Marriage is a blood covenant. We don't see marriage as a blood covenant, but God says it is.

> Malachi 2:13-16 - AMP "And this you do with double guilt; you cover the altar of the Lord with tears (shed by your unoffending wives, divorced by you that you might take heathen wives), and with (your own) weeping and crying out because the Lord does not regard your offering any more or accept it with favor at your hand.

> Yet you ask, "Why does He reject it?" Because the Lord was witness to the covenant made at your marriage between you and the wife of your youth, against whom you have dealt treacherously and to whom you were faithless. Yet she is your companion and the wife of

your covenant (made by your marriage vows).

And did not God make (you and your wife) one (flesh)? Did not One make you and preserve your spirit alive. And why (did God make you two) one? Because He sought a godly offspring (from your union). Therefore take heed to yourselves, and let no one deal treacherously and be faithless to the wife of his youth.

For the Lord, the God of Israel says: 'I hate divorce and marital separation and him who covers his garment (his wife) with violence.' Therefore keep a watch upon your spirit (that it may be controlled by My Spirit), that you deal not treacherously and faithless (with your marriage mate)."

Proverbs 2:16-17 - AMP "(Discretion shall watch over you, understanding shall keep you) to deliver you from the alien woman, from the outsider with her flattering words, who forsakes the husband and guide of her youth and forgets the covenant of her God."

When the bride and groom feed each other the wedding cake, they are saying symbolically, "I'm coming into you and you into me. We are becoming one." This symbolic union is made complete by the physical act of marriage when the groom and bride come together as husband and wife.

Exodus 20:14 - AMP "You shall not commit adultery."

1 Corinthians 6:18 - AMP "Shun immorality and all sexual looseness (flee from impurity in thought, word, or deed). Any other sin which a man commits is one

outside the body, but he who commits sexual immorality sins against his own body."

I Corinthians 10:8 - AMP "We must not gratify evil desire and indulge in immorality as some of them did —
and twenty-three thousand (suddenly) fell dead in a
single day!"

Galatians 5:19 - AMP "Now the doings (practices) of
the flesh are clear (obvious): they are immorality, impurity, indecency."

We wear the wedding ring on the third finger because
man believed that the third finger had a nerve leading to the
heart. And since the heart is the central part of the body that
keeps the blood circulating, it became the symbol of life.

We use the word "heart" to represent the total person.
It stands for your whole being, your whole nature, your whole
life. When you love someone with all your heart, you love
him with all your being. When you give your heart to someone, you are giving him your total life. This is the essence
and spirit of the blood covenant, which God ordains in the
Bible and that man has always recognized.

God requires the shedding of blood in all God-initiated
covenants. Both the old and new covenants required this
bloodshed. First were the animal sacrifices with Abraham,
consummating the old covenant, and then the precious blood
of Jesus on the cross to consummate the new covenant.

The first sexual union between a man and woman was
to be in the marriage covenant. The consummating of this
covenant, made with God for life, is by the shedding of blood.
Their blood covenant is consummated when the hymen is
broken. You see now why God says pre-marital and extra-
marital physical intercourse is sin.

Sadly this has little meaning today. Most people are not virgins when they marry. Recently a woman, who had been married more than once, told me she was unhappy in her current marriage. She already had two children but she and her current husband had none. Naturally they were not virgins when they married. They repented for past incorrect relationships and prayed and asked God to restore them, then had sexual relations. There was a showing of blood during those relations and she conceived and nine months later gave birth to a (covenant) child from God. Now isn't this an awesome story of the love, and the grace, and the mercy of God? His goodness sometimes overwhelms me. When these parents say "this is a special child", they mean truly special.

If you were sexually active before marriage, married before your current marriage, committed adultery, or were even molested, sexually, abused or raped, let's pray and ask God to heal and cleanse the defilement of the past. In a moment He can wipe away the dregs of the past. If you feel you need to talk to someone because you have been sexually abused, by all means do so. Sometimes there are wounded pockets in our souls and spirits that need special tending. But this prayer will spiritually cleanse you.

P
R
A
Y
E
R

Dear Lord, I come humbly before you, and ask you to forgive me for all sexual activity outside of my marriage. Forgive me for fornication, adultery, sensual and sexual teasing of males, and any other unclean act I may have indulged in, including foolish things that young girls can get into together. Father, I forgive anyone who ever harmed or hurt me sexually. I release them. I release my pain, my shame, and my anger.

(For those whose husbands left them) - Father I forgive my husband for forsaking me. I know this wasn't your plan, but heal us both, Lord. Heal my abandonment, displacement and the wound of betrayal. (For those who have been divorced) - Father forgive me for breaking my marriage vow and breaking my covenant with you. Thank you that your grace is sufficient to cover my sin. I praise you for this.

Father, in your Word You have given us full power over the enemy. You say, what we bind on earth is bound in heaven, so I bind all unclean spirits, all spirits of perversion, lust, adultery, fornication and whoredoms. I break the evil power of these spirits off of my life and my children's lives and the lives of their seed now living and the seed yet to come. I shut the door to these spirits and put the blood of Jesus over the door. Your Word also says that whatever we loose on earth, it is loosed in heaven. Therefore, I release an anointing of purity and restoration into my life and my family's life.

I break the power of all curses that have come into our lives and nail them to the cross. Lord, please cleanse all the defilement that's come into our lives and release generational blessings into our lives. I give you glory that you are the God of restoration and pray this in the Name of Jesus. Amen

3. The Miracle of the Scarlet Thread by Richard Booker, Destiny Image Publishers, page 27.

11

How to Minister to Your Husband Sexually

1 Corinthians 7:1-5 - AMP "Now as to the matters of which you wrote me. It is well (and by that I mean advantageous, expedient, profitable, and wholesome) for a man not to touch a woman (cohabit with her) but to remain unmarried.

But because of the temptation to impurity and to avoid immorality, let each (man) have his own wife and let each (woman) have her own husband. The husband should give to his wife her conjugal rights (goodwill, kindness, and what is due her as his wife), and likewise the wife to her husband. For the wife does not have (exclusive) authority and control over her own body, but the husband (has his rights); likewise also the husband does not have (exclusive) authority and control over his body, but the wife (has her rights).

Do not refuse and deprive and defraud each other (of your due marital rights), except perhaps by mutual consent for a time, so that you may devote yourselves unhindered to prayer. But afterwards resume marital relations, lest satan tempt you (to sin) through your lack of restraint of sexual desire."

G od had a plan and man has certainly defiled it. God is
calling us women to rise up and meet His standard in
marriage. God's intent was that a man's wife would
meet his sexual needs and desires and he would do the same
for her. How have things gotten so mixed up?

We can make an assumption by the size of families in
days gone by, that when a man came home from long hours in
the field, or a long journey, or the war, or the factory, he and
his wife (after dinner) got together sexually. This probably
happened more nights than not. It was a natural happening
in life. God intended it to be so! What happened?

Now sex is something played out on TV screens, in movies, in porno places, in magazines, in extra-marital affairs,
with unmarried couples, but not correctly played out in most
marriages. In marriages the bed has become the battleground
rather than the playground. God intended sex to be a good
thing, a fun thing, and an emotional and physical release for
both husband and wife.

Today people are so busy. In the majority of homes,
both husband and wife work. Most households have television, VCR, or music playing all the time. There is little time
for conversation. Children are involved in multiple extra-
curricular activities. They get home late, are exhausted and
need help with their homework. Many women have to do
housework and laundry in the evenings. Frequently, Dad is
horizontal on the couch watching his favorite sport while
Mom is doing all these things. Dad may be thinking, "I hope
she hurries up and gets the work done, I'm starting to get
tired. I don't want to be too tired for sex, but if she's not
ready in the next thirty minutes, I'm not going to make it.
Thirty minutes go by and he starts to drift off with an "oh
well". Or perhaps Dad is in the garage or basement fixing an
appliance and Mom is plopped on the couch watching her

favorite "romantic comedy", thinking, "Now why doesn't he treat me like that. I've been cheated in life. He just wants sex, but he doesn't know how to sweep me off my feet. Well, there is no sex for him tonight. I'll wait until he learns how to bring a little romance into our life."

How sad it must be for God to look at His creation and see how we have fractured the beautiful gift He gave us. In my examples, I was very kind. Many people have come to me for advice regarding their sexual problems and the reality is that God's glorious gift has become a curse and a burden far too often.

My request of you is that you would be totally honest with yourself. Look at the area of sexual intimacy in your marriage and measure it against the standard that God set in His Word. God feels it's important because the Holy Spirit breathed inspiration into Paul so that He could write this inspiration in the Holy Scriptures.

Paul writes, that it would be advantageous for a man not to marry, but he understood that there would be a temptation to impurity and immorality for those who did not marry. The reason that there would be a temptation is because God had placed in a man and in a woman a sexual drive. This is a normal thing, although sexual drives today are not frequently normal. Many have perverted drives, while many others have dysfunctional drives. God desires to heal all perversion and dysfunction and bring sexual drives into His divine order according to His divine plan.

So Paul's advice was for each man to have his own wife and each woman to her own husband. He told the husband to give his wife her conjugal rights and likewise the wife to her husband. Let's look at the word conjugal.

- ♦ Conjugal means of and relating to the married state or to married persons and their relations.

- ♦ Conjugal rights are the sexual rights or privileges implied by and involved in the marriage relationship.

- ♦ The right of sexual intercourse between husband and wife.

As we can see in the above definition, conjugal rights are the right for sexual intercourse. To my way of thinking, in order to make this fair, God stated in His Word first, that a husband was to take care of his wife's sexual needs before He stated that a wife was to take care of her husband's sexual needs.

It is important for a husband to take care of his wife's sexual needs. He is to be there to take care of her in every area possible. When a man will not meet his wife's sexual needs, it is devastating to her. It devalues her as a woman. It lowers her self worth. God placed within a woman that need for nurturing and intimacy. Sex to her is nurturing, closeness, intimacy, approval, belonging, acceptance, care-taking, etc.

When a wife will not meet her husband's sexual needs he feels deprived and angry. Because he needs release in sex, he sometimes (this is incorrect) begins to think of other ways he can get sexual release. Many times to a man sex is just sex, or sex is conquering, release, relaxation, etc. To her it is all about feelings and to him it's all about an act. But put the two together and you have the perfection. I see it as the sensitivity and the strength that God created.

Men need to work at becoming more sensitive to

women's needs and not just release and conquering. Women need to be aware of men's need to be released sexually. When a husband and a wife choose to care more about the other than they do about themselves, they will begin to enjoy sexual ecstasy. This is the way God intended it to be. We have become selfish human beings; living in a selfish society that is only concerned about getting their own needs met.

God also says that a wife is to meet her husband's sexual needs. God's plan was that a man would never have to go to anyone other than his wife to be sexually fulfilled. It is normal for men to have a powerful sex drive. God made them that way. They need to know that when they desire sex, their own wife will be ready to receive them. Sex should be a normal, regular part of marriage. A man or a woman should have the confidence that when they have sexual desires, they can freely go to their mate and that desire will be fulfilled.

Is your marriage this way for you? Do you believe the Word of God is true? Is it your desire to be obedient to the Word of God? Are you willing to be a doer of the Word, and not just a hearer of the Word? Are you going to be obedient or rebellious? Do you want to function in the Kingdom of Light or the kingdom of darkness?

James 1:22-25 - AMP "But be doers of the Word (obey the message), and not merely listeners to it, betraying yourselves (into deception by reasoning contrary to the truth). For if anyone only listens to the Word without obeying and being a doer of it, he is like a man who looks carefully at his (own) natural face in a mirror. For he thoughtfully observes himself, and then goes off and promptly forgets what he was like.

But he who looks carefully into the faultless law, the

(law) of liberty, and is faithful to it and perseveres in looking into it, being not a heedless listener who forgets but an active doer (who obeys), he shall be blessed in his doing (his life of obedience).

Let's study some more of our scripture verse. It says do not refuse, deprive and defraud each other. That means do not withhold sexual intercourse from one another. Husbands and wives must stop refusing each other what is due and stop denying or depriving one another. Of course if you both agree to abstain for a time for fasting and prayer that is scriptural. Our picture is made complete as we look at the dictionary definitions of the following words.

♦ Refuse means avoid, shun, to decline to have as a husband, deny

♦ Deprive is to take away, remove, destroy, to take something away from

♦ Defraud is to take or withhold from one some possession, right, or interest by calculated misstatement or perversion of truth, trickery or other deception.

So many times married couples deny sexual intimacy. They offer excuses such as, "I'm too tired", they pretend to be asleep, promise tomorrow for sure honey, pick fights right before bedtime, say "I'm coming to bed soon" and then stay up until they're sure he or she is asleep, or flat out have such lousy relationships that the thought of sex isn't even in the picture. Worse yet is the couple who treats each other horribly, no kindness, no tenderness, no warmth, no caring and

then when bedtime comes sexual relations are expected. Now according to the Word these relations should not be denied, but it takes a super abundance of God's grace to have sexual relations with one who treats you horribly.

A woman should be willing to minister to her husband sexually. Most of the women I know, have an understanding that they have a responsibility to minister to their husbands, (especially if she is not working, but at least to share in if working), to provide meals, clean clothes, house clean enough to live in, conversation, child tending, etc. This is all part of her ministry to her husband. But ministering to him sexually is equally as important. Pray and ask the Holy Spirit, your teacher, how to minister to your husband sexually. Every man is different, every relationship is different and only the Holy Spirit can reveal truths to you about your man, your special man. For some this may seem very intimidating. Fear not, the Holy Spirit will also be your step-by-step guide.

What I'm trying to impart in this book is how to change even the worst marriage into a marriage of love, commitment, joy, peace and ecstasy. This may seem like a big order, but nothing is too big for God.

If you feel the sexual part of your marriage is lacking, you need to begin to believe God to change it for you. He is ready, willing, and more than able to work on you, and on your husband. The Word tells us that as we sow, we will reap. It is imperative that as women we sow right seed into our marriages. The hardest, meanest, man can be won over by soft and gentle words. In the Word, God tells us to love and submit to our husbands. Submitting in sex may not be easy. Can you look at your husband as the very special gift of love God gave to you, (even if your gift is a little rough looking now), and know you can do this as unto God? Your willingness to be obedient will be the platform God is going to use to change him. Will it take a miracle for you to be able to do this? God is in the miracle working business! Allow the following scripture to deeply penetrate your heart, and remember we are to be doers of the Word and not just hearers of the Word.

> 1 Peter 3:1-2 AMP "In like manner, you married women, be submissive to your own husbands (subordinate yourselves as being secondary to and dependent on them, and adapt yourselves to them), so that even if any do not obey the Word (of God), they may be won over not by discussion but by the (godly) lives of their wives, when they observe the pure and modest way in which you conduct yourselves, together with your reverence (for your husband; you are to feel for him all that reverence includes: to respect, defer to, revere him and, in the human sense, to adore him, that is, to admire, praise, be devoted to, deeply love, and enjoy your husband)."

You may think that is too large a task. As we read the Word and meditate on it and pray the Word, we become what the Word says. The Word is alive and is able to change and mold us into His image and likeness. This is God's idea, not mine nor yours. So if God said it - it's possible. God has changed everything in my life and hundreds of others that I've worked with. He wants to change things in your life too. Submit and yield yourself to Him, cry out to Him, HELP, HELP ME LORD, CHANGE ME LORD! I have a friend who wears a pin that says, "try God". That's what I want to say to you, "TRY GOD"!

Our scripture ends with the statement that after prayer and fasting resume marital relations lest satan tempt you to sin through your lack of restraint of sexual desire. The passions of man's or women's flesh are to be willingly met in marriage. As Christians, even if our sexual desires are not met in marriage, we have the fruit of the spirit of "self control" and we are able, through God, to control ourselves until God changes our situation. A couple that has a satisfying sexual life does not go elsewhere looking for sex or any other fulfillment. Apply the Word of God. God knows the perfect plan for marriage — he created it. He knows what is needed between husband and wife. Trust Him.

The culture and customs of today's society portray sex as anything but a pure and holy thing between husband and wife. But you are in a new culture now, with new customs, a new mandate, and a new Leader. You are part of the Christian Culture, with Jesus Christ as your Leader and the Word of God as your mandate. So whatever is in your marriage that does not fit under the Lordship of Christ, you can have the confidence that as you submit yourself to Him, and are obedient to all that He shows you, He is willing and able to help you change.

Are you willing today to trust Him? Some changes come quickly, but most change takes time. Remember our goal is to become "one" in marriage. Becoming "one" sexually is part of becoming "one". I personally believe this is very important in the eyes of God. Lay down your past hurts, your past mistakes, your past ignorance, and your control in this area, or even being a victim in this area, please pray the following prayer.

P
R
A
Y
E
R

Dear Lord, this seems like an almost impossible task to me, but I know that with you, all things are possible. I can do all things through you who strengthens me. I want to submit to you and lay on your altar of sacrifice the sexual intimacy part of my marriage. Forgive me for all the times that I did not correctly minister sexually to my husband. I choose to forgive him for all the time he did not correctly minister sexually to me. God you created sex and to you it is a beautiful thing. Give me eyes to see the same beauty that you see in sex. Father, blow up the mind sets and structures and patterns that I have about sex. I turn in my old scrapbook of all my hurts and disappointments and acts of revenge, etc. I place the blood and the cross over all of this. I cry out for a complete transformation in the area of sex, a transformation by the hand of Your Spirit, not by my hand.

Holy Spirit be my teacher in this. You know exactly what my husband's needs are and what my need's are, so please guide us and lead us in this area. My total hope and trust is in you Lord. I will not put expectations upon my husband, but will believe you to work in his life too. Right now I want to be changed. Change me Lord. Do not allow me to look at him while you work on me. I choose to die in every area that will harm our marriage and our sexual intimacy. Make me the wife that he needs and desires. Lord I love you for caring about all these areas in our lives. You are so good to us. I give you praise and glory for this in the name of Jesus. Amen.

12

Reverence Your Husband

1 Peter 3:1-2 - AMP "In like manner, you married women, be submissive to your own husbands (subordinate your- selves as being secondary to and dependent on them, and adapt yourselves to them), so that even if any do not obey the Word (of God), they may be won over not by discussion but by the godly lives of their wives, when they observe the pure and modest way in which you conduct yourselves, together with your reverence for your husband: you are to feel for him all that reverence includes:

- To respect, defer to, revere him - to honor, es- teem, appreciate, prize and in the human sense, to adore him, that is, to admire, praise, be de- voted to, deeply love, and enjoy your husband.

Now isn't that a tall order? But once again we have to remember we can do all things through Christ who strengthens us.   Note: It says in verse 1, "in like manner", or the NKJ version says "likewise". Verse seven to the husband says "in the same way you married men should live considerately with your wives". The NKJ version says, "husbands, likewise dwell with them with understanding, giv- ing honor to the wife". God is very fair; He expects husbands and wives to treat each other with honor. But in every section of the Bible that teaches on marriage, the wife submitting always comes before the husband loving and dying. So, I see this as, wives be obedient to the Word, and function in Godly submission, and God will honor His Word and bring the rest to pass".

IS YOUR MAIN GARDEN THRIVING OR IS IT WITHERING?

Your husband needs to be nurtured. Every living thing needs nurturing if it is to continue to grow, bloom and live. The more nurturing and tending, the more every living thing grows. It's fall now, and I've planted some new mum plants. One planter has a double planting of beautiful pale purple mums. Another planter has an enormous planting of large golden yellow spider mums. Every time I pass by them, I smile. Live flowers make me happy. I feel that they are such a gift from God. We moved into a condominium two years ago preparing for Richard's retirement next year. But moving into this condominium did not stop me from planting flowers around my entrance, or from having other beautiful containers of flowers around my entrance and on my balcony. I take very good care of these plants. My husband, sons, and grandchildren (when they are around), all help me water and care for these beautiful plants. Our condo association doesn't keep up the grounds the way they should, so I tend to the grounds surrounding our condo. My neighbors just said the other evening that they planted some mums and weeded their area, because when they looked at ours, they saw how nice it was. When we go away, we hire someone to come and water our flowers. If we didn't, we know that they would all wither up and die while we're gone. Have you ever

come home from a trip and looked at your plants and saw them all dead? That has happened to us in the past, and it is very discouraging.

This may seem like a silly, simple story, but it gives a picture of how important it is to water, care for and tend to living things. Let's now look at our husbands. If we are able to care for flowers, (and God cares for flowers too), how much more should we care for, tend to, water with attention, and love our husbands.

You may be thinking, "If you only knew how impossible this is going to be for me to do. He is so inattentive to me or he is so mean, or he wouldn't like that. He doesn't like attention". First of all, even the most impossible situations, are possible with God. Secondly, the Word says, "As we sow we will reap". So even the meanest or most inattentive man cannot undo the law of sowing and reaping. This is a Spiritual Law of God that is just as relevant and just as powerful as the Law of Gravity. Third, as I address the comment that he doesn't like attention, I'd argue that he acts like he doesn't like attention. Maybe at some point in his past he was hurt or rejected, even by you, or something has caused him to be insecure. There is a root to the reason he is acting like he does not like attention.

Everyone responds to attention. Attention, care and interest, properly given, not in some phony, sickening way, will start a process of melting the hardest heart, bringing to life the deadest soul, and energizing the meekest and quietest man. The glorious other side of it all, is that when you begin to sow into your marriage seeds of nurturing, and you forget about yourself, you will be planting a crop that will bring forth a harvest for you! Isn't God just too good? We always say, "Our God is good, all the time!"

LORD, HOW DO I
REVERENCE MY HUSBAND?

We must always be focused on the fact that we are to be doers of the Word, not just hearers of the Word. These two facts, properly applied in all areas of our lives, will make us glorious overcomers.

Remember the Holy Spirit is our teacher. He will teach us specific things to do for our husbands. They're all different. What God has me do may be very different from what He has you do. Look at the meanings of reverence and ask God to give you practical applications.

- Respect: An act of noticing with attention; consideration; the quality or state of being esteemed; courtesies; to look toward or at; interest in

- Defer to: To refer or submit for determination or decision; to submit or yield through authority or respect; yield

- Revere: To regard with reverence or profound respect and affection; practice an affectionate deference toward; show love and honor to

- Honor: Outward respect or admiration; recognition; a person of superior standing or importance (he's the priest and king of your home); one that is of intrinsic value; to show high regard or appreciation for; to treat with consideration

- Esteem: Approval and respect often blended with great liking or fondness because of worthy qualities; to set a high value on; hold in high regard

- Appreciate: To evaluate highly or approve warmly often with expressions or tokens of liking; to be admired and highly valued; to esteem highly and express thanks or gratitude for

- Prize: To regard as exceptional or great worth or excellence; esteem highly; hold as highly desirable or very precious; appreciate the value

- Adore: To regard with reverent admiration; to esteem or love often with an accompanying outward expression of such regard; to be extremely fond of; to be deeply attached to, often to the point of excess

- Admire: To regard with wonder or astonishment; to regard with wondering esteem, accompanied by pleasure and delight; regard with an elevated feeling of pleasure; to take pleasure in; to like and enjoy

- Praise: To determine the worth of; commendation for worth or excellence; approval expressed; honor extended because of excellence or worth

- Devoted to: Consecrated to a purpose; ardent and zealous

- Deeply love: The attraction, desire, or affection felt for a person who arouses delight or admiration or elicits tenderness, sympathetic interest or benevolence; devoted affection for

- Enjoy: To feel or manifest joy; have a good time with; to take pleasure or satisfaction in; to make happy

We look at a word like reverence and think that shouldn't be too hard to do. But when we see what it really means, one could be tempted to throw her hands up into the air and give up. "But God!" Isn't it wonderful that we know a miracle working God who cares about us and cares about our marriages? Our God is willing to give us all the grace we need, and then give us all the help we need to be a doer of the Word and "reverence" our husbands.

God desires that every Christian wife understand this truth and make it real in her life. Not enough women are treating their husbands this way. When you start treating your husband this way, everyone around you will take notice. They'll see something in your marriage that isn't in theirs. They'll want what you have.

This is going to take time. Ask God to help you prioritize your time. You need time to nurture your own husband and to minister to his emotional needs. Now would God have said to reverence our husbands, if He did not know that they needed to be treated reverently? Most marriages are not where God wants them to be, because the woman is not willing to reverence her husband. He's not number one in her life after God. Remember as you sow, you will reap. (No sowing, no harvest.) Remember, in the Bible, where God gives instruction in marriage, He designates for the woman to cooperate first. Won't you cooperate with God?

Take each definition of reverence and write down as many practical things as you can think of to apply to your situation with your husband. Remember, if you get stuck, your teacher, the Holy Spirit will help you. You are not alone in this. Take it slow and easy. Be obedient to each thing God shows you and before long, you will see a miracle right before your eyes. The first miracle will be in you. As you are obedient, God will so change you and so change your heart. Then naturally and continually the love and reverence God wants you to have for your husband will begin to flow out of your heart.

> **P** *God, as I look at the word reverence and all that it means, and as I realize you said that I am to*
> **R** *reverence my husband and to feel for him all that the word reverence includes, I am humbled.*
> **A** *I know without You I could never do this. But with You, all things are possible. I give you my-*
> **Y** *self and my plans and my desires. I want your plans and your desires. God teach me through*
> **E** *the daily anointing of Your Holy Spirit how to continually reverence my husband. Thank you*
> **R** *for the gift you have given me in my husband. Please forgive me for not being the wife he re-*
> *ally needed. Forgive me for not nurturing him and for not planting and not weeding his gar-*
> *den. I will trust you to show me how to meet his emotional needs. God allow me to sow good*
> *seed, so that I will have a plentiful harvest. Most of all though Lord, I want to do this because I*
> *love you and want to be obedient to you, in Jesus' name I pray. Amen*

13

Your Words ...
Bitter or Sweet Water?

We can learn a lot about the tongue in the book of James.

James 3:1-12 - NKJ "My brethren, let not many of you become teachers, knowing that we shall receive a stricter judgment. For we all stumble in many things. If anyone does not stumble he is a perfect* man, able also to bridle the whole body. Indeed, we put bits in horses' mouths that they may obey us, and we turn their whole body. Look also at ships: although they are so large and are driven by fierce winds, they are turned by a very small rudder wherever the pilot desires.

Even so the tongue is a little member and boasts great things. See how great a forest a little fire kindles! And the tongue is a fire, a world of iniquity (unrighteousness). The tongue is so set among our members that it defiles the whole body, and sets on fire the course of nature: and it is set on fire by hell. For every kind of beast and bird, or reptile and creature of the sea, is tamed and has been tamed by mankind.

But no man can tame the tongue. It is an unruly evil, full of deadly poison. With it we bless our God and

Father, and with it we curse men, who have been made in the similitude (likeness) of God. Out of the same mouth proceed blessing and cursing. My brethren, these things ought not to be so. Does a spring send forth fresh water and bitter from the same opening? Can a fig tree, my brethren, bear olives, or a grapevine bear figs? Thus no spring yields both salt water and fresh."

* Perfect - Teleios Strongs #5046 - That which has reached an end, that is, finished, complete, perfect. When applied to persons, it signifies consummate soundness, and includes the idea of being whole. More particularly, when applied to believers, it denotes maturity.) [4]

Matthew 15:11-18 - NKJ "Not what goes into the mouth defiles a man, but what comes out of the mouth, this defiles a man. But those things which proceed out of the mouth come from the heart, and they defile a man."

Proverbs 4:23-24 - NKJ "Keep your heart with all diligence, for out of it spring the issues of life. Put away from you a deceitful (devious) mouth, and put perverse lips far from you."

I have personally found that this is one of the key areas in every woman's life that needs sanctification. And I know that most men need this area sanctified too. This problem is common to both genders. Both my husband and myself needed our mouths saved, sanctified and restored. We were born-again, filled with the Holy Spirit, and yet had to work diligently with God for the sanctification of our mouths.

It is hard to believe that we can love God, serve God,

want to please Him in every way, and still have something happen that will stir up the bitter water that is in the cistern of our hearts. And, of course, the entire issue here is our hearts. We use the word heart so loosely. I noted in chapter 10, when we speak of the heart of man, we are not speaking of the physical heart chamber within our bodies. What we are talking about is the core or the essence of man. Our hearts are made up of our soul and our spirit. When we are born-again our spirit is immediately saved, but our soul is saved daily. We all know the following scripture:

> Philipians 2:12-13 - NKJ "Therefore, my beloved, as you have always obeyed, not as in my presence only, but now much more in my absence, work out your own salvation with fear and trembling for it is God who works in you both to will and to do for His good pleasure."

Our souls are our minds, our wills, and our emotions. Throughout life and many times throughout marriage, there is much damage to our emotions. We may never have learned to submit our wills to anyone, so when our husbands desire something from us, our will rises up. Everyone's mind is different. Many things, through the course of life, happen to damage our minds. That's why the Word tells us we have to renew our minds in the Word of God. As we renew our minds in the Word, we begin to become that portion of the Word that we take in or ingest.

> Hebrew 4:12 - NKJ "For the Word of God is living and powerful, and sharper than any two-edged sword, piercing even to the division of soul and spirit, and of joints and marrow, and is a discerner of the thoughts and intents of the heart."

The more we allow the Word of God to impact our lives and change us, the more our minds are renewed. In 1989, I purposed with God that I would cooperate with Him and His Word to have my mouth changed, by allowing Him to change my heart. I no longer wanted bitter and sweet water flowing from my mouth. Every word that comes out of our mouths produces something. Life or death.

Proverbs 18:20-21 - NKJ "A man's stomach shall be satisfied from the fruit of his mouth; from the produce of his lips he shall be filled. Death and life are in the power of the tongue, and those who love it, will eat its truth."

If we find ourselves talking harshly, or speaking anything that does not edify God, something in our heart is causing this type of conversation. Is it hidden anger? How about an old wound and a root of bitterness hidden deep within our hearts? Something has suddenly sprung up to the surface and it must be dealt with.

As wives we have to be so careful. A woman can actually spend a great deal of time working on sanctifying her marriage and reverencing her husband one half or two thirds of the time and the rest of the time tearing him down with her mouth. Life and death are truly in the power of the tongue.

(For every negative thing that we might say, it takes saying twelve positive things to balance out our negative communication.)

Bitter water is usually poisonous. There may only be a small amount of a contaminant in the water that turns it bitter, but drink enough of that bitter water a little at a time, and

you will get sick. One thing for sure, you won't be going back on a regular basis for much more of that water. So it is with our husbands. If their communication with us results in drinking bitter water, they quickly learn that they'd rather be thirsty than to take a chance on getting another drink of bitter water.

Examine your times of communicating with your husband during the last six months. During your conversations, has sweet or bitter water flowed? Now, I perfectly understand that he may be giving you bitter water to drink. But the Word we are allowing to change us tells us:

Proverbs 15:1 - NKJ "A soft answer turns away wrath, but grievous words stir up anger."

Try your best not to react to bitter words that might be coming from your husband. You can be the catalyst to bring healing to both of you.

In 1989, as I allowed God to change my conversation by changing my heart, wonderful things began to happen in me, in my home, and in my relationships. My conversation became pleasing first of all to God, then to my husband, my family and to those all around me. I became quieter, and more settled. The more I observed what came out of my mouth, the more I could quickly go to God, asking Him "What was in my heart that allowed this to come forth?" It took many months of diligently seeking God for me to get victory in this area. But within myself, I had a determination that I wanted sweet water and blessing to come forth out of my mouth.

I studied the scriptures on the mouth and heart and meditated on their meaning. I would cry out to God to change me. He knew I was serious about this and that I would cooperate with Him. The problem with a lot of Christians is that they pray one prayer, go on their merry way and expect to be changed. So many times, change requires something from us. We have to cooperate with God. If we are sincere, and cooperate with God, He will more than help us to be set free.

If you want God to change your mouth, so that sweet water will flow from it, and if you desire blessing and not curses to come forth from your mouth, please pray the following prayer.

P
R
A
Y
E
R

Dear Lord, thank you for your great love for me. Thank you that with your help, I can become an overcomer. I ask you to sanctify my mouth. I do not want sweet water and bitter water both to flow from my mouth. I want to be a blessing to my husband and to my family. Thank you that your Word is living and powerful and sharper than any two-edged sword, and that it pierces even to the division of soul and spirit, and of joints and marrow. Thank you that it is a discerner of the thoughts and intents of the heart. Lord sanctify my heart. I will cooperate with you and trust you to deliver me by the power of Your Blood and the power of Your Spirit every time that you show me the nasty things that are in my heart. Thank you that Your Blood covers my sin and that You forget my sin as far as the east is from the west. Father give me the grace to forgive myself for my areas of sin. I give you praise and honor for changing me in Jesus' Name I pray. Amen

4. Spirit Filled Life Bible, New King James Version, Thomas Nelson, Inc., Word Wealth Pages 1898-1899.

14

The Gentle Flow of Godly Communication

B eing able to communicate correctly is essential if we are going to be "one flesh". If we do not talk with one another and if neither husband nor wife tells the other how they feel about the issues in their lives, how can we become one? So many times women think they have to stuff everything and cannot express their opinions. This is not so. A huge reality in life is, "it's not what you say, but how you say it". So we want to talk about how to communicate in a godly manner.

Now we know that very few men are "real communicators". The majority of men like to drop facts and that's it. Women, on the other hand, like to really talk things out. Many times a woman likes to talk all around a subject, just to work out her thoughts. That kind of talking really frustrates a man, because he wants to hear facts, period.

A woman needs to learn how to communicate in a godly manner. We know God gave wives to men be their helpmeets. So if a decision is to be made, a woman is to give her input, including any warnings she may feel she is hearing from God. The thing a woman can't do is force her husband to follow her advice. She needs to give input and then back out. Our position is to go to God and ask God for His perfect will to take place in the decision. As women, the thing we have to understand is God sometimes allows a wrong decision to be made so He can work on our husbands. Always, always, we must do everything as unto God, and trust God at all times in all situations. Many times the answers to our prayers have to be worked out in a way we would never choose. But God knows what is best for all of us.

Sometimes there are unresolved issues in our lives. We call these issues "sacred cows". These are areas that everyone steps over and no one wants to open up, because there is a knowing that when this issue is opened up it won't be pleasant. But if we are to be "one", then we are going to have to talk about these "sacred cows". If they are left alone long enough they will start leaving some nasty deposits in our lives, (just like the real cows). My own experience has been that my husband never really liked it when I would open up the issue. If I dropped it and prayed to God for Him to bring about His perfect will, in both my husband and myself, I would be rewarded with the issue being resolved right before my eyes.

If I felt I had to keep talking and arguing about the issue, then I would see my husband shut down and we would get nowhere. We must always remember that God is the third person in our Marriage Covenant. When we leave him out of our communication, we leave out the most important person. The Word tells us that we are to speak gently when we speak. Let's look at some scriptures.

Proverbs 15:1 - NKJ "A soft answer turns away wrath, but grievous words stir up anger."

Proverbs 15:4 - AMP "A gentle tongue (with its healing power), is a tree of life, but willful contrariness in it breaks down the spirit."

Proverbs 25:15 - AMP "By long forbearance and calmness of spirit a judge or ruler is persuaded, and soft speech breaks down the most bonelike resistance."

Proverbs 16:13-14 - AMP "Right and just lips are the delight of a king, and he loves him who speaks what is right. The wrath of a king is as messengers of death, but a wise man will pacify it."

Now let's look at our marriage scripture and compare it to the above scriptures.

1 Peter 3:1-6 AMP "In like manner, you married women, be submissive to your own husbands (subordinate yourselves as being second to and dependant on them, and adapt yourselves to them), so that even if any do not obey the Word (of God, they may be won over not by discussion but by the (godly) lives of their wives, when they observe the pure and modest way in which you conduct yourselves, together with your reverence (for your husband; you are to feel for him all that reverence includes: to respect, defer to, revere him-to honor, esteem, appreciate, prize, that is, to admire, praise, be devoted to, deeply love, and enjoy your husband).

Let not yours be the (merely) external adorning with (elaborate) interweaving and knotting of the hair, the wearing of jewelry, or changes of clothes; but let it be the inward adorning and beauty of the hidden person of the heart, with the incorruptible and unfading charm of a gentle and peaceful spirit, which (is not anxious or wrought up, but) is very precious in the sight of God.

For it was thus that the pious women of old who hoped in God were (accustomed) to beautify themselves and were submissive to their husbands (adapting themselves to them as themselves secondary and dependent upon them). It was thus that Sarah obeyed Abraham (following his guidance and acknowledging his headship over her by) calling him lord (master, leader, authority). And you are now her true daughters if you do right and let nothing terrify you, not giving way to hysterical fears or letting anxieties unnerve you)."

The Word tells us a woman who has a gentle and peaceful spirit also has an incorruptible and unfading charm. Our scripture also tells us a man can be won by your godly life as they observe your pure and modest ways. We can take this to many levels. The first level, and probably the most important of all, is that unsaved husbands will be won to the Lord by their wives' conduct.

The second level is a man who is born again but not following God, will be won over by his wife's chaste behavior; her gentle and peaceful spirit. There is a holy jealousy that comes over a man when he sees his wife so changed. Suddenly he begins to hunger and thirst for what she has. This is all part of God's plan from the beginning.

The third level is God has provided an opening for communication through a quiet, gentle, and peaceful woman. A woman who opens up communication with a determination to do whatever it takes to win, is not what I'm talking about. Have you heard a woman called a "Jezebel"? Jezebel was a queen in the Old Testament who controlled everyone and everything in her path. She did whatever it took to get what she wanted. She knew how to be forceful, how to manipulate and how to control. What we find in women is they have

often come through some very hard circumstances and they have learned to rely on no one but themselves. Their lack of trust has caused them to fear. Their fear then propels them into control.

When they open up a "sacred cow" they mistakenly feel, "this is my only chance, so I'm going to get it all in". They go after their issue with both barrels. In effect, they become God in their life. When we do this God will sit back and allow us to get nowhere. Worse yet, things often get worse. Then, when we finally trust God and do it His way, He is ready to do a work in our lives that will blow us away!

If we can all get a picture of this it will change our lives. We can trust God and let Him work things out in His own way, in His own time, or we can keep on going around the same mountain over and over again. Remember God has given us freedom of choice. My prayer for you is that you will make the right choice and trust God.

One of our noted scriptures tells us that a soft answer turns away wrath, but hard words stir up anger. Now we know God's Word does not lie. So if it says hard words are going to stir up anger, they are going to; just as it says a soft answer turns anger away, the soft answer will drive away anger. This is a choice that, as it is laid out for you, will cause you to be a doer of the Word one way or another. For me, the more I consistently chose to be a quiet and gentle spirit and spoke softly, not wanting my way, but wanting God to come and intervene in ALL the circumstances in my life, the more this manner became securely deposited in me. We are to become obedient and choose, and then He implants the truth in us. I don't understand His way, but I know I love His way!

Another text scripture says there is healing power in the tongue. The healing power in our tongues can bring healing that is like a tree of life, (a reviving tongue). That same tongue is capable of breaking down and tearing down the very spirit of a person. If a woman is bent on controlling everything in her home, and if she wants everything her way, and if she consistently beats down her husband, she will break his spirit. Can you imagine what an abomination it is to God when we do this to the one He says is Priest and King of our homes?

Another scripture shows us there may be a very difficult situation the family is facing. If a woman has long forbearance and calmness of spirit and soft speech, without manipulation, even the meanest and hardest person will be won to God's view on things. There are women whose husbands are not born again, but because of the beautiful spirits of these women, their husbands are godly priests of their homes. (They just don't know it yet.)

I believe a quiet and gentle spirit is a major key on the road to "one-flesh". In order for "one-flesh" to take place in a marriage there has to be correct alignment in the marriage. That alignment is your man standing tall as head of your home with you fitting perfectly in his side; the place you were taken from.

If you feel you are lacking in this area and you want God to change you, pray the following prayer.

P R A Y E R

I can surely see I have a long way to go. Please forgive me for trying to control my husband. God, I want to do this your way. I bind the spirit of control and command it to loose me. I bind all familiar spirits of control and command them to loose me. I shut the door to these spirits and break their power generationally and break their power off of my seed and me. Father I ask you to loose a submissive spirit in my life. I break the power of all curses that my actions have brought into our lives. Father teach me how to be a quiet, gentle, and peaceful woman. I desire my husband to be won over by my godly conduct. Lord, I know I could never do this on my own, but with you all things are possible. Father I ask you to now to release generational blessings into our lives, in Jesus' name I pray. Amen.

15

Establish Yourself in Faith

Romans 10:17 - NKJ "Faith comes by hearing, and hearing by the Word of God."

Romans 12:3 - NKJ "For I say, through the grace given to me, to everyone who is among you, not to think of himself more highly than he ought to think, but to think soberly, as God has dealt to each one a measure of faith."

Matthew 17:20 - NKJ "So Jesus said to them, 'Because of your unbelief; for assuredly, I say to you, if you have faith as a mustard seed, you will say to this mountain, "move from here to there," and it will move; and nothing will be impossible for you.'"

Many times as God begins to change us we have a tendency to think, "I'm changing, what about him? Is this fair God? Why do I have to do all the changing or why do I have to do all the dying?" If this is you, don't be discouraged. Almost everyone goes through this from time to time. It's really important that you establish in your heart that God is in control and God is going to change your marriage into a "glorified marriage". It's imperative for women to go to the Word of God and get all the scriptures on marriage securely hidden in their hearts. Faith truly comes by hearing the Word of God, ingesting the Word, and then chewing on that same Word until that Word becomes a living part of the individual.

When I began to stand for my marriage to change, I remembered from my youth religion classes that we ALL have the measure of faith that is the size of a mustard seed. I also remembered as that seed was watered and cared for, the plant grew up to be one of the largest ones in the garden. So, as I stood for my marriage, I would think about my having that mustard-seed faith. Every time I prayed, every time I loved, every time I served, every time I reverenced, every time I obeyed, every time I prayed God's Word concerning my marriage, my planting of faith was growing. Before long I had a supernatural faith that could not be moved and I knew God was not a man that He would lie, but He would do all that He promised in His Word and even more.

I began to see that I could speak to those mountains in my life and command them to move. I also had a revelation that I did not have to make anything happen. I only had to believe with unmoving faith that God would do it. After all, He is the Alpha and the Omega; the beginning and the end. He is the author and the finisher of our faith. A godly marriage is in the center of God's heart. He truly desires this for us. All we have to do is trust him without fear. As we learn to trust God working in our lives, even when it doesn't look like it, we become Sarah's daughters.

1 Peter 3:1-6 AMP "In like manner, you married women, be submissive to your own husbands (subordinate yourselves as being second to and dependant on them, and adapt yourselves to them), so that even if any do not obey the Word (of God), they may be won over not

by discussion, but by the (godly) lives of their wives, when they observe the pure and modest way in which you conduct yourselves, together with your reverence (for your husband; you are to feel for him all that reverence includes: to respect, defer to, revere him—to honor, esteem, appreciate, prize, that is, to admire, praise, be devoted to, deeply love, and enjoy your husband).

Let not yours be the merely external adorning with (elaborate) interweaving and knotting of the hair, the wearing of jewelry, or changes of clothes; but let it be the inward adorning and beauty of the hidden person of the heart, with the incorruptible and unfading charm of a gentle and peaceful spirit, which (is not anxious or wrought up, but) is very precious in the sight of God.

For it was thus that the pious women of old who hoped in God were (accustomed) to beautify themselves and were submissive to their husbands (adapted themselves to them as themselves secondary and dependent upon them). It was thus that Sarah obeyed Abraham (following his guidance and acknowledging his headship over her by) calling him lord (master, leader, authority). (And you are now her true daughters if you do right and let nothing terrify you, not giving way to hysterical fears of letting anxieties unnerve you)."

Sarai, (her name wasn't changed to Sarah yet), was asked by her husband Abram to follow him because God had told him to leave his country, leave his family and leave his father's house and go to an unknown land God had prepared for them. Then Abram tells Sarai that God spoke to him about giving great lands to his and Sarai's descendants. Naturally this caused Sarai to do a double take because they had no children and were far beyond childbearing age. But Sarai willingly followed her husband. Then her husband made a bad decision. He asked her, (because he was afraid that the Egyptians would kill him and let her live,) to say she was his sister so it would be well for him because of her and they'd let him live. Sarai was taken to Pharaoh's home and Abram was treated well because of her. But God was not happy with Abram's decision. (God has a way of dealing with our husbands and showing them truth when they are in error.) He plagued Pharaoh and his house with great plagues. Pharaoh became very angry with Abram and asked him why he lied about Sarai, when she was really his wife. (Pharaoh had been considering taking her for his wife.) Pharaoh and his men then sent Abram away.

I do not know why Sarai didn't say, "I won't lie for you". It appears that even though she was unhappy, (she knew this could cause great problems for her if Pharaoh insisted on taking her for his own), her trust and faith in God was greater than all of her circumstances. Abram had told a half-truth, as Sarai was his half-sister. I would never tell anyone to do anything that would go against God's Word. Our assumption has to be that she had the peace of God, in her submitting to her husband's wishes. They key for all of us, is to hear God and be obedient to Him.

Many years went by and Sarai and Abram still had no children. God took Abram and showed him the stars in the sky and told him his descendants would be as the stars. Abram believed God and God accounted it to him as righteousness. (You see, if we will just believe God for the things He's promised, even though they look impossible, He will account it to us as righteousness also.)

Now we come to the part where Sarah takes her eyes off

of God and decides she needs to help things along. She tells Abram to go into her maid Hagar because God has restrained her, Sarai, from having a child. Sarai influenced Abram, (as Adam had been influenced by Eve) and he went into her maid and Ishmael was conceived. Then Sarah becomes jealous of Hagar and Hagar runs away. The situation got messier and messier.

This is so typical of situations in many people's lives. They hear from God. They know it is the voice of God. Yet, if he does not come through and produce His promise as quickly as they think, they try to produce the answer. When one is not content to wait on God, and starts murmuring and acting restless, the devil sees these actions and puts a suggestion in one's mind that looks good, sounds good and is certainly something they are capable of producing. Once a person takes their circumstances into their own hands, and tries to produce the answer, God backs away. He says, "they have to learn the hard way", and lets the individual try to work it out. Parents often do this with their children, when the child insists on going their own way. Whenever an "Ishmael" comes into one's life, there is usually something leftover that has to be dealt with for a long time, sometimes forever.

If you've taken things into your own hands and taken your eyes off of God, do not despair. We serve an awesome God who will keep on coming around and giving us another chance to focus on Him. He is so good. Our goal should be to get it right as quickly as we can.

When Abram was almost 100 years old, God reaffirmed His covenant with Him, (after he and Sarai learned a few things, just like the rest of us). God then changed his name to Abraham because he was the Father of many nations. (Calling those things as not, as real, before they were.)

Romans 4:16-17 - NKJ "Therefore it is of faith that it might be according to grace, so that the promise might be sure to all the seed, not only to those who are of the law, but also to those who are of the faith of Abraham who is the father of us all (as it is written, I have made you a father of many nations) in the presence of Him whom he believed-God, who gives life to the dead and calls those things which do not exist as though they did."

Then God changed Sarai's name to Sarah. God said he would bless her and give her a son and she would be a mother of nations and kings of peoples would come from her. At this time Sarah was 90 years old. (Nothing is impossible with God.) And as we know, in spite of it all, Sarah did conceive a beautiful son, Isaac. Even though there was a long period of time from the promise to the fulfillment of the promise, God was faithful. Please let that sink in. God is faithful, what He says He's going to do, HE WILL do.

God is calling women to be Sarah's. Perhaps you are the first one born-again in your family. Maybe God has a plan for multitudes to be affected by your salvation. That's how it's been with me. What God has done since I said yes to Him all those years ago has astounded me.

Following are some points about Sarah:

+ She was a mother of nations.

+ She was a beautiful example of a married woman.

+ She was unique, beautiful, brilliant and creative.

- Sarah was unequivocally devoted to Abraham.

- She shared his challenges and heartaches and his dreams and blessings.

- She stood by his side through thick and thin, hard times, and blessings.

- Sarah loved and honored Abraham in her youth and in her old age.

- Her love was unconditional and tenacious.

- Sarah was by nature strong willed, but chose to submit to her man.

- She and Abraham truly understood the meaning of "one-flesh".

Let us follow Sarah's glorious example, letting nothing terrify us and allow us to give away to hysterical fears and anxieties; to be women who humbly submit to our husbands; trust God completely, and also to have a sincere commitment to nurture and pass on what we know to the following generation(s).

Hebrews 11:1-11 - NKJ "Now faith is the substance of things hoped for, the evidence of things not seen. For by it the elders obtained a good testimony. By faith we understand that the worlds were framed by the Word of God, so that the things which are seen were not made of things which are visible.

By faith, Abel offered to God a more excellent sacrifice than Cain, through which he obtained witness that he was righteous, God testifying of his gifts; and through it he being dead still speaks.

By faith, Enoch was taken away so that he did not see death and was not found because God had taken him; for before he was taken he had this testimony, that he pleased God. But without faith it is impossible to please Him, for he who comes to God must believe that He is, and that He is a rewarder of those who diligently seek Him.

By faith Noah, being divinely warned of things not yet seen moved with godly fear, prepared an ark for the saving of his household, by which he condemned the world and became heir of the righteousness which is according to faith.

By faith Abraham obeyed when he was called to go out to the place which he would receive as an inheritance. And he went out, not knowing where he was going. By faith he dwelt in the land of promise as in a foreign country, dwelling in tents with Isaac and Jacob, the heirs with him of the same promise; for he waited for the city, which has foundations, whose builder and maker is God.

By faith Sarah herself also received strength to conceive seed, and she bore a child when she was past the age, because she judged Him faithful who had promised. Therefore from one man, and him as good a dead, were born as many as the stars of the sky in multitude-innumerable as sand which is by the seashore."

If you want to follow in Sarah's footsteps, please pray the following prayer:

P
R
A
Y
E
R

Dear Lord, I am choosing today to trust You. I am willing to leave my place of comfort and follow my husband as you lead us on a journey of new life in our marriage. I know that he will make mistakes, as I know I will make mistakes. I thank you, Lord, that Your grace is present to enable us to pick ourselves up and start all over again. I refuse to believe the lie of the enemy, when he'll try to tell me this isn't going to work. I trust you to do a work in me that will enable me to be like Sarah. Thank you that I will be a beautiful example of a married woman, that I'll share my husband's challenges, heartaches, dreams and blessings. I will love my husband now and through our old age. Thank you that my love will be unconditional and tenacious. Enable me to let nothing terrify me, and I purpose to not give way to hysterical fears and anxieties. I proclaim that I will humbly submit to my husband, and I also will share with and teach others what you show me, in Jesus' name I pray. Amen.

16

Home is Where Our Hearts Are

Titus 2:1-5 - NKJ "But as for you, speak the things which are proper for sound doctrine, that the older men be sober, reverent, temperate, sound in faith, in love, in patience, the older women likewise, that they be reverent in behavior, not slanderers, not given to much wine, teachers of good things, that they admonish the young women to love their husbands, to love their children, to be discreet, chaste, homemakers, good, obedient to their husbands, that the Word of God may not be blasphemed."

It used to be that it was fairly normal for all young women to have some homemaking skills. They used to teach some homemaking skills in high school. We have found in our encounters with women in the last few years that many do not have a clue as to how to take care of their homes and their families.

I want to paint a word picture for you that I hear all the time. Women are buried under mountains of dirty laundry. They feel their irons are to be used for bookends. They never have all of their dishes, pots, and pans clean at the same time. The health department could possibly condemn the bathroom. The bedroom has one narrow path to walk through on the way to the rumpled bed each night. The dining room table and the kitchen table are piled high with newspapers, mail, books, cereal boxes, and hamster cages. The living-family room is a disaster. Everyone's shoes are left at the front or back door (or both). Coats, hats and sweaters are strewn all over the chairs, couches and floor. There's some half folded laundry on the end of the couch. Half eaten sandwiches, pizza, cookies and apples are on the tables. Games are everywhere and the toddler has almost all of his toys deposited at various places around the room. It's 4:30 in the afternoon and our happy homemaker starts to think about dinner. Suddenly panic hits her. She has not taken anything out of the freezer to prepare for dinner, neither has she even thought about what she wants to make. As she racks her brain for ideas, she realizes that everything she thinks of, she can't make because she doesn't have the ingredients. Once again, for the 100th time that day, total defeat and failure hits her. She cries, "I'm hopeless, this is hopeless; oh God help me, help me."

She calls the local pizza place again for a quick delivery and prays a quick prayer to God, "Forgive me Lord, I promise, tomorrow I'll try to get it together better". She goes to bed exhausted, without her children bathed and no clean clothes for school the next day, wakes up the next day and repeats it all. The kids are fighting, the homework isn't done, she doesn't have bread to make their sandwiches for lunch, nor does she have lunch money for them. She quickly thinks, "I wish I hadn't gone to Mc Donald's for lunch yesterday. If I hadn't gone, I would have had enough money for their lunches." One child is screaming, "You didn't sign my permission slip". She frantically signs the slip, hands them each two Granola Bars - one for breakfast and one for lunch.

After they leave, she sits the baby down in front of the TV and takes out her Bible. She asks God to help her get it together. She recognizes that she needs help. He takes her to the Passage above in Titus 2:1-5. As our young mother reads this she realizes that she can go to a woman in her church that is older than her, humble herself and ask for help. She knows that even though her husband isn't on her case (all of the time), this is not making him happy. She senses how he frequently distances himself from her. He never brings anyone home or invites anyone over. She wonders, "I'm sure he's embarrassed to ask anyone over." Then she remembers, "I'm so lonely because I never ask anyone over or bring anyone home, because I'm embarrassed." Her head goes down in shame. Then she senses the small inner voice of the Holy Spirit, saying, "go to the Women's Bible Study at your church, and let them know your desperation. Humble yourself and ask for help." This excites her as it's a confirmation of what she felt earlier. Hope that she hasn't felt in a long time fills her heart.

Now, we all know her state of desperation is not God's best for her. God knew there would be some who would be struggling with their responsibilities as homemakers, because he made provision for their getting the help they need in the Word. God admonishes the older women in the Bible to equip the younger women. When I was having a leadership meeting for our ministry I mentioned that all of us are older than someone. One of our thirty something women said she had a heart for the young girls after they graduate from high school and college. It seems this is a ripe area for ministry in the church.

Those of us who are spiritually mature, the phrase older woman has nothing to do with age, but is referring to the spiritually mature woman, need to become mentors to the struggling younger women. This is best done in a non-threatening, non-structured atmosphere, such as in the spiritually mature woman's home. The time is to be spent nurturing, training by example, teaching new skills, sharing each other's lives; and then the spiritually mature in the role of spiritual mother, imparts spiritual truth. This is God's plan, not my plan, not your Pastor's plan or even your plan. Then the mentor can begin to hold the younger woman accountable for growth in the areas they're working on. This type of spiritual mothering is so powerful and so rewarding. I truly believe that there is a special anointing for this type of teaching and training.

The following is a true story. A beautiful Christian woman in our church, (a spiritual mother), had four young women over one day. One of the girls was her daughter who had her two-year-old son with her. That day, they made homemade noodles, learned how to make bread, and also how to make the perfect apple pie. They all shared stories and experiences and learned much in the process. This lovely woman knew that one of the girls was struggling, a lot like the girl mentioned above. She took the struggling girl aside and told her that she had struggled the same way when she was young. My friend's exposing of her own shortcomings when she was young set the younger woman at ease.

When these four younger women went home that day, they each took with them, a freshly baked loaf of bread, a large bag of homemade noodles and a perfect apple pie. All four were thrilled. It was like they had been given a priceless gift. My friend was completely exhilarated. She knew that somehow that day; she had touched the heart of God. Not only had she blessed and mentored these young women, but she had spent time with her daughter and her grandson. She also had the blessing of a loaf of bread, a bag of noodles and a perfect apple pie for her own dinner. Five households were blessed that afternoon. Imagine, one act of mentoring blessing five households. I don't think it gets much better than that. All five women felt they had been born for what they were doing that day. The effect of that day has borne permanent fruit in the lives of those young women.

When people are desperate and feeling they have no hope, sometimes just knowing someone else has been where you are helps. Also, just knowing other women want to fellowship with you, makes you somehow know you are okay. If you are really struggling, ask someone to come along side you and help you.

I have found it is better to do this at the spiritually mature woman's home. The reason for this is that the younger woman sees how to do it in an environment that is not so overwhelming. Also, the goal is never to go and do it for them, but to teach them how to do it. You know the old saying. "If a man is hungry and you give him something to eat, he has a meal, but if a man is hungry and you teach him to fish, he can eat for a lifetime."

Of course our harried homemaker has to go home. What does she do then? We still use our same principles we've been using. We are to be doers of the Word. She has to begin, in her home, one room at time, one discipline at a time. She needs to study the diligence scriptures and read the Proverbs in the Bible. As she begins to sow into these areas she will soon begin to reap a harvest. There are some things she will feel she does not know how to do. She has her teacher, the Holy Spirit. The Holy Spirit will guide her, direct her, and surely help her. Continuing with the above story, I want to relate how this happened to our young friend who was struggling with her home.

She was so inspired that she asked the Holy Spirit, where do we start. He told her the bathroom. She spent a whole day there. Her husband was shocked when he came home.

He started insisting that the whole family become neater and cleaner in their bathroom use. Then she gets out the crock-pot and every day has dinner ready when her husband gets home; sometimes there is even homemade bread. One night her husband came home and said, "Are you going to leave me?" She assured him she wasn't and that she wasn't cooking him his last meal.

After that he came home excited about the surprises she was going to have for him. I asked her to speak about her victories to a group of woman. She sat down with God and said, "let's talk God, I want to get this holiness thing right, and I want to know what you want me to say tomorrow." She sat piously waiting to see where in the Bible God was going to take her. He said, "let's go into the kitchen, I want to clean the kitchen today." So all day, she and God cleaned and rearranged the kitchen. As they rearranged the kitchen, God rearranged her. She had a glowing testimony I had her give twice the following day.

Her husband is completely taken by all of this. One day, he began to weep and said, "All I want is all that God wants for me." She was astounded. This had been her heart's cry for a very long time.

All of this is to show how important it is to take care of your home. If it weren't important to God, He wouldn't have made reference to it in the Bible. God has a plan to get you help, through a godly older woman. But when there is not an older woman to help you, the Holy Spirit is always there. When I had twins almost 29 years ago, I came home from the hospital to four boys under five years of age. I began to cry out to God, to teach me how first to survive and then how to get organized and how to do all that I had to do. He was faithful to teach me and to this day, I still employ many of the things He taught me.

How does this fit into oneness and "one-flesh"? A man works very hard to provide for his family. He and his wife are on the same team. He has a portion to do, as she has a portion to do. If both work, naturally there is a different distribution of chores. A man desires to come home to a clean house, the children clean and dressed nicely, groceries purchased, and dinner made.

Rome was not built in a day. Start working on this, one area at a time. Watch how this begins to bring you and your husband closer and closer. He may even jump in and help with more at home as he watches your efforts. Many times they should be helping, but when they see such chaos, they don't feel like doing anything either.

If you're ready for change, pray the following prayer.

P
R
A
Y
E
R

Dear Lord, I need help. I try and try, but I never seem to get anywhere. I'm going to trust you to help me conquer this insurmountable appearing mountain in my life. Forgive me for not doing it all right in the past. Please show me who to ask to help mentor me. Holy Spirit please teach me all I need to know to be a happy fulfilled homemaker. I want to be a doer of the Word. I want to be a keeper at home. Thank you for producing this in me. Amen.

17

"A Virtuous Wife" More Precious Than Jewels

Proverbs 31:10 - AMP - "A capable, intelligent, and a virtuous woman - who is he who can find her? She is far more precious than jewels and her value is far above rubies or pearls."

To find a good wife (and also a good husband) is a good thing. Whenever we go to weddings, we need to pray that God will bring each couple into the blessed state of "one flesh". Couples speak their vows, but often don't fully understand what they mean, or how to fulfill them. A woman is to be that jewel for her husband, she is to be the jewel in his crown. Every woman should desire to ignite joy in her husband's heart. How sad that so many women do things that expose their husbands and bring shame upon them. Some women find it great sport to talk about their husbands with others and to expose their husband's nakedness. The thing women who do this don't realize is that they are exposing themselves also, because they are one with their husbands. The reality is, what damages their husbands, damages them too.

Proverbs 12:4 - AMP "A virtuous and worthy wife (earnest and strong in character) is a crowning joy to her husband, but she who makes him ashamed is as rottenness in his bones. "

Proverbs 18:22 - AMP "He who finds a (true) wife finds a good thing and obtains favor from the Lord."

When a woman is true, to her husband, she and her husband obtain favor from the Lord. If you are not experiencing favor from God, maybe you need to ask God if you are being true to your husband in every area.

- True - steadfast, loyal, honest, just, truthful, and accurate

Proverbs 31:11 - AMP "The heart of her husband trusts in her confidently and relies on and believes in her securely, so that he has no lack of (honest) gain or need of dishonest (spoil)."

He knows that she will do nothing to hurt him, harm him, embarrass him, or in anyway cause him shame.

Proverbs 19:14 - AMP "House and riches are the inheritance from fathers, but a wise, understanding, and prudent wife is from the Lord."

The Result

Proverbs 31:23 - AMP "Her husband is known in the (city's) gates, when he sits among the elders of the land."

And those who see and admire this man have an inner knowing that not only is he to be honored and respected, but his wife also . My husband is a greatly honored and respected man, by his family and friends, in his church, at his place of

employment and by his business associates. He truly is known in the city's gates, when he sits among the elders of the land. God had this plan for him and God was very interested in me cooperating with Him, so the purpose and destiny of both of our lives could be fulfilled. God's heart cry in marriage is "one flesh". He's speaking over us, "My daughters, please just cooperate with me and my plan so that my purposes can be fulfilled on the earth and My Son can come back for the Church, His Bride." Our cry has to be "yes Lord!"

What Does Virtuous Really Mean?

- Strong's Definition: Chayil #2428 - Wealth, virtue, valor, strength, great forces, goods, host, weight, power, riches, substance, valiant, valor, war, worthy.[5]

When you look at these words, you can quickly see that each word describing virtuous depicts it as powerful and weighty. Don't you want to be a virtuous woman? I do.

- Dictionary definition of virtuous is - Potent, efficacious, having or exhibiting virtue, morally excellent, righteous, chaste.

- The definition of virtue is - conformity to a standard of right, morality, a particular moral excellence, a beneficial quality or power of a thing. Chastity especially in a woman.

Today, as I think about the women and girls I come into contact with through the media, work, life and even church, it appears that many do not understand the meaning or value

of being chaste.

- ♦ Chaste - Pure in thought and act - modest

Let's examine the area of dress. Is Jesus blessed by the way you dress each day? It's so important that we correctly display and sanctify the Lord each day of our lives. There is much to be said about modesty. I don't believe in skirts only, no make-up or hair in a bun, but we do have to be careful that we don't lower our standards to the low standards of the world today. When someone sees us their first reaction should be, "there is something so different about her, I want what she has." We honor our husbands when we dress in a chaste, modest fashion. You still can wear stylish, lovely, brightly colored clothing and certainly jewelry. Ask your teacher, the Holy Spirit, if He approves of your dress. He will answer you and help you. Also, God desires our actions to be pure, so pure that both God and our husbands are being sanctified correctly through our actions.

Another area that women have to be careful in is discretion. You have to be careful to not say things about your husband or your family that you will regret later.

- * Discretion - Having or showing discernment or good judgment in conduct and especially in speech. The ability to make responsible decisions.

As women, there comes a point when we are functioning in all the things we are learning in this book:

- ♦ Our husbands will trust us.
- ♦ They will rest in the fact that we would not make

decisions that would displease them.

+ In their hearts they will know we would not talk negatively about them around others.

+ They can spend their time at rest, in peace, because they know that they and their wives have become "one".

If you desire to be this virtuous woman, please pray the following prayer:

P
R
A
Y
E
R

Dear Lord, once more, I cry out for change. I don't want to do this half way, but I desire to do this completely and wholly. I want to be a complete blessing to my husband. I desire him to be able to be at perfect rest knowing that I will only do him good and not harm all the days of our lives. Cause me to be a woman of discretion. My desire is to be chaste in my dress and in my actions. Lord, your Word says that your desire for us is that we would live life as "one-flesh" with me securely placed back into that place inside and alongside my husband from which woman was taken from Adam. How this works is a mystery that only you understand, but I trust it to be so in my life. Thank you that you have worked this out in our lives in Jesus' name I pray. Amen.

Conclusion
"Conforming to a Right Standard

A s Christians we know God's Standard of Right is His Word. So as we have been looking at what the Word says about Woman and her role and position in marriage, our goal has been to discover just what is really necessary to become a Virtuous Woman, a Virtuous Mother, and a Virtuous Example for other women to follow.

As you've been going through this book and applying the godly principles to your life, you have probably found there have been seasons of great change. Change is wonderful. We are daily to change more and more into the image and likeness of Christ. Some change is painful, some joyful and some downright difficult. But remember the end result is glorious. God knows the beginning and the end. He has a glorious plan for your life.

Galatians 6:9 - NKJ tells us "Do not be weary in well-doing for in due season you will reap a harvest."

Know that as you begin this, it will be your sowing time. There is always seedtime and harvest. How can you expect a crop, unless you sow your seed? We have to always remember that the seed is the beginning of a great harvest. If you keep your eyes upon the Lord and not on your mate, and if you ask God to change you, and allow Him to change your mate, you will be well pleased with your harvest. Expect a plentiful harvest. It's God's grace and love coupled with your obedience that will change you, so please allow that same grace and love of God to change your husband. Notice: God can do it. He doesn't need your help. Rest in this as you continue your journey of change!

My prayer for you is that everything in this book will become a reality for you. Marriage is most important to God. Marriages here on earth are microcosms of the marriage that Jesus desires to have with His bride, the Church. One day soon Jesus will return for the Church. He won't return until the Church is ready. But when He does return, He will take His Bride, the Church and make her one with Him. He will take His Bride and put her back into His Side and the Church and Christ will become one. What a glorious thought!! We add our prayer to the prayer of John in the Book of Revelation. "Even so, come, Lord Jesus."

The End

Bibliography

1. Personality Plus, Florence Littauer,
    Baker Publishing

2. Women's Study Bible,
    N. J. Nelson Publishers, Page 1615

3. Miracle of the Scarlet Thread,
    Richard Booker,
    Destiny Image Publishers, Page 27

4. Spirit Filled Life Bible,
    New King James Version,
    Thomas Nelson, Inc. Publisher,
    Word Wealth, Pages 1898 - 1899

5. Strongs Exhaustive Concordance of
    the Bible,
    Riverside Book and Bible House,
    Hebrew and Chaldee Dictionary,
    Page 39

Has your life been changed by this book?
I'd love to hear your story.
Please contact me at:

Issues of the Heart
PO Box 1183
Crown Point, Indiana 46308

or

www.issuesoftheheart.com

Also, a great companion to this book is:

"Hope for Change"
Step-by-step Plan for raising Morally responsible,
Happy, Likeable Children —
from Infancy until they Leave the Nest"

Order from
www.issuesoftheheart
or
www.amazon.com